# The Great Record Promoter
## Behind the Scene in the Record Industry
### Memoirs of Linda Wills

# The Great Record Promoter
## Behind the Scene in the Record Industry
### Memoirs of Linda Wills

# Linda Wills

| Library of Congress Control Number: | | 2015900237 |
|---|---|---|
| ISBN: | Hardcover | 978-1-5035-3278-6 |
| | Softcover | 978-1-5035-3279-3 |
| | eBook | 978-1-5035-3280-9 |

Print information available on the last page.

Rev. date: 06/03/2015

**To order additional copies of this book, contact:**
Xlibris
1-888-795-4274
www.Xlibris.com
Orders@Xlibris.com
670319

# CONTENTS

Dedication.................................................................................................vii
Acknowledgments.......................................................................................ix
Introduction...............................................................................................xi

## PART ONE
## GROWING UP IN WASHINGTON, DC

1. Family Life ........................................................................................3
2. Tragedies – from JFK to MLK—That Affected my Life .........................12
3. Inner City Living ..............................................................................14
4. My Greatest Losses ..........................................................................21

## PART TWO
## LIFE WITH A SUPERSTAR

5. My Amazing Love Affair....................................................................27
6. Working for Green Enterprises...........................................................31

## PART THREE
## WORKING FOR TEDDY PENDERGRASS

7. The Road Secretary...........................................................................41
8. Ride or Die Friends ..........................................................................43

## PART FOUR
## BEHIND THE SCENES IN THE RECORD INDUSTRY

9. Internship .......................................................................................51
10. Record Promotions ..........................................................................53
11. Conclusion ......................................................................................64

Praise For Linda Wills........................................................................65
Index.................................................................................................67

# DEDICATION

This book is dedicated to my mother Elaine T. Wills and my family.

# ACKNOWLEDGMENTS

I want to first make reference to and thank my Lord and Savior Jesus Christ for the grace and mercy that He has given me. Next, I want to thank my wonderful mother Elaine Wills, who was and continues to be the pillar and strong tower throughout my life. Thank you dad for your love and inspiration. To my brothers, thank you Jamie for being a protective big brother and looking out for me when I was growing up; thank you Cornell for teaching me how to fight to protect myself; thank you Melvin, you inspired me to want to work in the music industry working as secretary with your group the Royal Tones; thanks Everett and Mark for your love and wisdom. Thank you James my only child (you are gone to soon) for being my greatest inspiration. To you Jazsmon, my granddaughter I could never tell you enough how much I love you. To my grandson Delonte you are a wonderful person and I love you very much. Hammurabi Bey, thanks for being a true friend and mentor for me through the years. To my twin nieces Tia and Mia, thanks for being my geek squad. Thank you, Tom Mabry for being a good friend and supporting me for the past 40 years. You have introduced me to so many people who have inspired my life. Michele thank you for everything, I appreciate you. To you Morgan my assistant thanks for being there whenever I need you. Thank you, Annette for being a true friend for the past 20 years. Thank you, T Greene for making me the girl of your dreams and for being a die heart friend. Thomas I can't thank you, Eric, Phil and Hartwell enough for your support. To my aunts, uncles, nieces, nephews and cousins I will always love and appreciate you.

A very special thanks to my uncle Maury Wills, Cathy Hughes, Doug E. Fresh, Salt-n-Pepa, Darryll Brooks, Roy Ayers, Mark Wills, and Pastor Jones for your kind words that describe me as a person and a record promoter.

# INTRODUCTION

My life has been filled with success, failure, happiness, sadness, and occasionally, devastation, but through it all I have persevered and through my faith, I have come to appreciate the accomplishments I have been blessed with. I owe a great deal to the many individuals who have helped me throughout my life. The section GROWING UP IN WASHINGTON, DC is designed to demonstrate that individuals are formed by their early communities. I was blessed with 5 brothers, a mother, and a father who worked diligently to help us all succeed. This was no less true of my extended family: the community that also raised me. I remain amazed at the sheer genius and creativity of those I have been fortunate to have met throughout my life and career. As with many of us, I have lived a life—while not always entirely of my choosing—that has been a blessing and something of a demonstration of that proverbial cliché: everything happens for a reason. I am in part, writing this book to share with you what little wisdom I may have learned throughout my career, and my hubris permitting, I hope to in some way leave something for the next generation of would be promoters. It is with that sentiment that I begin my journey, a journey that could not have been possible without the guidance and grace of the Lord, who I first and foremost wish to thank for his goodness and mercy from which all blessings flow. He has been my protector, refuge, and place of safety from dangers seen and unseen and his love continues to guide me.

I have always been captivated by the record industry. Having the good fortune to work in the industry I love, I found it to be everything that I thought it would be and so much more. I have traveled across the United States living the "rock-and-roll lifestyle," first as a personal secretary for a superstar and later as a record promoter for record companies and distributors. Most of my forty-year career has been spent working behind the scenes, rendering an invaluable service, supporting artists and record companies. The mostly unseen and demanding work of a record promoter is often overlooked but her presence may become the difference between making recording artists superstars or making an average song a hit.

This book is a memoir of my life. In these pages I discuss my upbringing in Washington, DC and its influence on my career in the record industry. It is with humility and a little trepidation that I write these words, but hope that they will provide some small insight and lessons for freshmen and veterans of the industry alike and in the process perhaps provide some entertainment to you the reader.

I have had the great pleasure of working for or with some of the country's most talented and gifted artists including: Al Green, Teddy Pendergrass, Smokey Robinson, Roy Ayers, Salt-n-Pepa, Tupac Shakur, Doug E. Fresh, EPMD, Gerald LeVert, D-Train, David Bowie, Bobby Womack, Johnny Taylor, H. B. Barnum, H-Town, Luke (aka Luther Campbell), and many other entertainers. It is with great appreciation for these colleagues and friends that I write this memoir.

# PART ONE

# GROWING UP IN WASHINGTON, DC

The Wills Family

# CHAPTER ONE

## Family Life

**M**y early life prepared me for many of the challenges I would face in the music industry. I am the product of my family's rearing, and I believe that their influence provided me with the power to sustain, to preserver, and to deport myself in a decent and sensible manner. In the 1950's my parents moved to a project development in southeast Washington, Barry Farms. Decades prior to that, Mr. James Barry had owned the Barry Farms property, which in the 1800s, he sold to the Freedmen's Bureau, who parceled it out as settlements for freed slaves. A large percentage of Barry Farms was sold at the behest of the Redevelopment Land Agency. We lived in a three-bedroom row house. It was spacious, with a midsize kitchen, dining room, pantry, living room, and coat closet. Our recreation center had an outdoor swimming pool with a lifeguard, but because I didn't take swimming lessons, I played in the shallow part of the pool where I could stand up and walk around in the water.

My brother Cornell took me to the pool one day to teach me how to swim. He told me that he was going to ride me on his back through the water. As he was swimming, with me on his back, he suddenly ducked down into water and I was no longer on his back. I panicked and tried to swim on my own, but I couldn't get the rhythm of my hands and feet, so I started to sink. Of course, my brother played the hero and saved me after almost drowning me, but he thought that I would have learned to swim out of desperation. The fear of learning how to swim that day haunted me for many years.

Nor did I always know how to dance but was finally exposed to it when my oldest brother Jamie decided that he was going be my dance teacher. I can laugh now but those early days were anything but easy, and I was certainly not a natural. I wanted to be with my friends who could dance so I had to stick it out through some painful adolescence tears and frustrations, and because of the persistence of my brother I learned how to dance. I remember a lot of dancing at those parties – a cultural influence that, at the time escaped me as to its critical influence to my profession. I got so good at dancing, I joined a tap-dance group. The lady who lived on my street, Laverne Hamilton, cousin to R&B singer Billy Stewart, taught me how to tap dance. My dance group would perform, on stage, at St. Elizabeth Hospital, a psychiatric institution, and entertain the patients. The hospital was next door to the neighborhood and separated by a fence.

I fondly remember playing on the hospital grounds near a shady wooded area. The fruit trees provided plenty of shade and nourishment for that matter. One of the white male patients from the hospital would come down to the bottom of the hill to play with the neighborhood children. He was kind and gentle. One day, my friends and I took a shovel and dug a huge hole in a pile of dirt that was piled at least 20 feet high, and we made the hold large enough for us to climb into and sit down. It looked like an igloo so we called it our clubhouse. There was a railroad track at the bottom of the hill where the trains parked and unloaded their cargo: coal the fuel that we used to heat our homes. When I wasn't playing with friends I was playing by myself.

Since I was the only girl in the house I played with my baby dolls and imaginary mirror friends, Gibe and Jarbe. I sat in front of a large six foot mirror that stood against the wall in our living room playing by myself for hours. Every time, Mom came home from the hospital, after having a baby, she came home with a baby boy. I would cry and asks God, "Why did you make me the only girl in the family?" I decided to make my girlfriends, who were my neighbors, my "play sisters." While being the only girl often left me feeling like the black sheep in the house, it taught me at an early age how to be independent and to take things for what they are worth. There would come a time when I would wonder where were the female promoters in the record industry as well?

While our neighborhood was not as affluent as some, we were very close knit with neighbors often serving as surrogate families. We depended on each other, and in many ways our neighbors became part of a larger extended family which we relied on to care for and help one another. We were our brothers' keepers. If an adult saw a neighbor's child breaking the rules and misbehaving, the adult had the right to discipline that child as the surrogate parent.

Every family in the neighborhood had a common denominator and it was the fact that all of the families were receiving public assistance from the Welfare Department. Once a month, each family received a large box of American cheese, powdered eggs, peanut butter, powdered potatoes, and powdered milk. The families that had a lot of children received welfare checks and food. Let me tell you, we ate plenty of grill cheese sandwiches and that welfare cheese tasted good. We took peanut butter and jelly sandwiches to school for lunch almost every day. One of my neighbors had 11 children 10 boys and one girl. That family received the food and a check. Whatever food surplus the government was giving to aid the poor in this country, we were grateful to receive. This was years before the government started giving vouchers or food stamps.

Most families hope for better housing and schools for their children to attend. Parents worked hard to free us off of welfare. Circumstances as they were, many families in our neighborhood had to survive with the resources available to them – that in most cases meant government aid. And we had gardens. We once contracted poison ivy from all of the green vegetation that grew in the neighborhood.

Some of the folks in my neighborhood created their own revenue base and there were various hustles. I clearly remember a fair amount of "number backers" in the neighborhood. Number backers typically went house to house, collecting number slips and money from neighbors so they could put their numbers in for the day. The entire system was predicated on the outcome of horse races. If the numbers matched the winning horses for that day, you got paid. As far as I could tell, the street number business seemed to be quite lucrative for those running the racket. The money backers (and the people who hit the numbers) used the money to help support their families. If anything, this was probably a precursor to today's lottery.

Many of the things that were done back in the day seem to have been modified for today's use. Folks had "waistline parties" where they charged a sum equivalent to your waistline measurement. At the rent parties, they sold food and drinks and used the money to pay the rent to keep the family from being set out on the street. Other hustles were after-hour clubs, gambling joints, whorehouses, and bootleggers (people who sold liquor, after hours, out of their homes). Most of the liquor stores closed at 11 pm. Hustling was often turned to by good people, out of desperation; it was a way to feed families. People participated in those things because they had to improvise and find ways to make ends meet when they had low or no paying jobs. Even in those circumstances, I found myself exposed to the first inkling of the American entrepreneurial spirit. I think black people, are some of the best improvisers in the world; we have learned to make a way out of no way. My family's (the Wills) motto was: Where there is a Wills, there's a way. Growing up African American in the Nation's Capital had its pros and cons but we survived.

Barry Farms was an all-black neighborhood; we had one corner grocery store owned by a white family. Mr. Wallace, the neighborhood barber, used his home as a barbershop to cut hair for the boys and men in the neighborhood. Mr. Wallace was handicapped and couldn't walk; but he got around in a wheelchair. The candy lady sold candy, cookies, sodas, potato chips, and other snack foods out of her house. The ice cream man was a fine looking brother who worked for the Good Humor Ice Cream Company. When he drove through the neighborhood, ringing his bell, all of the children would run to their parents and ask for money to buy ice cream. When the ice cream man came around in the neighbor all of the kids were excited to see him because everyone loved ice cream and it was affordable.

The produce man, whom we called the husky man, rode in a wooden wagon pulled by a horse. His wagon was loaded with fresh fruits and vegetables for sale. He would yell, "Get your ice-cold watermelons." He always seemed to have a cold, juicy, sweet slice with black seeds already cut and waiting for us to sink our teeth into. The milkman picked up the recycling milk bottles left in the metal box on our porch, and replaced them with fresh, cold bottles of white milk. The coal man had baskets of coal and wood for sale. We had coal stoves that burned coal or wood for fuel to heat our homes. On the back porch of every house were large coal bins that were used to store the wood and coal and protect them from the rain and snow. We loved the coal bins. We sat on top of them and played. At night, we would lie back on top of the coal bins, under the light of the moon and stargaze at the beautiful, lit-up sky filled with stars. We could see the Big Dipper, Little Dipper, Ursula Major, and other constellations clearly. We didn't have to leave the neighborhood for much; we had all that we needed right in our community.

Our main shopping area was located on Nicholas Avenue. The Safeway Grocery Store, movie theatre, police precinct, Miles Long Sandwich Shop, the fire department, bakery, cleaners, liquor store, shoe shop, churches (Matthew Memorial Baptist and Campbell's Methodist) and Curtis Brothers' Furniture store were within walking distance. Curtis Brothers' built the world's largest wood chair to advertise and promote their furniture business. People came from miles around to see the chair. At one point, they built a glass house and placed the house on top of the chair. A white lady lived in the house. She kept the curtains open during the day and at night she closed the curtains before going to bed. She lived in that glass house for at least six months.

At one point my family really had a dry season, and things looked insurmountable, but Mom kept the faith. She never gave up on herself or my father's abilities to find better higher paying jobs. Once Mom went to cook dinner for us, and when she looked in the kitchen cabinets and the pantry everything was bare. I knew at that moment she felt like the character Old Mother Hubbard. When she looked in the refrigerator, all she saw were four large onions in the vegetable tray. She knew we had to eat something to keep from starving so she boiled and seasoned the onions with salt and pepper and we ate them. My brothers and I didn't complain; we knew that our parents were doing their best and that better days were ahead. My grandfather bought groceries to the house sometimes and we were glad to see him when he showed up.

Even though I wear designer clothes and shoes today, there were times when I've worn shoes with holes in the bottom and run-over heels. I remember walking to school in the rain and my feet got soaked and wet by the time I got to school. The corrugated cardboard used as an insole was wet and fell a part in the shoe. Some days, I wore my Mom's clothes to school after she left the house to go to work. A lot of my clothes came from the second hand stores (Goodwill or the Salvation Army), but I was glad that I had something to wear. Finally, my aunt Patricia, my mom's sister, started buying clothes for me. She bought me pretty dresses, skirts, blouses, tee-strapped patent leather shoes, and bow ribbons for my hair. I was once shy, lonely, and lacked confidence because I had to wear tattered clothes and raggedy shoes. When Auntie started dressing me I began to feel empowered and had a zest and zeal for life. I didn't look and feel like little orphan Annie anymore. My Mom took us to church on Sunday because she wanted us to grow up as good Christians. She taught us to be patient and to trust that God was going to give us the desires of our hearts with better days ahead. We learned early in life about the trinity (the Father, Son and Holy Ghost). I stayed in faith and God delivered me from a great deal of despair.

My parents never had to pay medical bills because we seldom got sick back, in the day. My mom gave me and my brothers a teaspoon of cod liver oil with a slice of orange every morning and we stayed heathy. If we seemed a little sick, she would give us a teaspoon of castor oil to clean out our systems. The most sickness people had were the chicken pox, mumps and the measles. She rubbed us down in calamine lotion to stop the itching. Mom made sure we had all of our vaccinations. To this day, I still have some traces of having had the chicken pox because they left spots on my arms from scratching when I itched.

When I was thirteen year old, still a youth, a nineteen- year-old man in the Navy proposed to me, and he asked my Mom if he could marry me. She thought that he had lost his mind or he was kidding. I was a teenager, tomboy, virgin, and certainly not ready for marriage. As a matter of fact I didn't even like boys at that age. If my dad had found out about this guy wanting to marry me he would have put that poor guy in a choke hold that would have killed him. My dad didn't allow me to date until I was seventeen years old. I was lonely growing up because I wanted a sister younger or older to play with.

My aunt Betty Jean would spend the night with me on the weekends sometimes and we enjoyed each other's company. One day, when I was visiting with Betty, at my grandmother's house, she sent me to the store, across Lincoln Park, to buy some ice cream. When I came out of the store, I lost my sense of direction and panicked. I threw the ice cream on the ground out of frustration and started to cry. Thank God, I saw a policeman walking the beat. I stopped him and told him that I was lost. He called for a patrol car to pick me up and take me to the Women's Bureau to wait for my parents to come to get me. I learned a valuable lesson that day and quickly soon after learned my parents' and grandparents' addresses and phone numbers.

My parents were a stickler when it came to keeping a clean house. They taught my brothers and me how to be team players and work as a team to clean the house. Mom taught us how to scrub, wax, and shine the wood floors in our home. We used Johnson paste wax to shine the floors. My brothers would sit me on a sheet and pull me across the floor, multiple times, and the friction from pulling the sheet across the floor would shine the wax on the floor. I had to thank God many times for not getting a splinter in my butt from being pulled around on the wood floor. Sometimes, we tied cloths around our shoes and skated across the floor over and over again until the floor started to shine. We had to take turns washing the dishes. If my dad came home late and the dishes were still in the kitchen sink, he would wake us up, regardless of the time, and make us wash the dishes. I stood at that sink many times at 2:00 o'clock in the morning, crying and washing the dirty dishes.

I learned how to wash clothes at an early age. I used a wooden metal scrub board to scrub the clothes clean. I starched my dresses, blouses and skirts with Argo starch; it gave the clothes a fresh look and made it easier to iron out the wrinkles. I hung my clothes on the outside clothesline to dry. The fresh air and the warm sun dried the clothes and gave them a fresh clean smell. Mom also taught me how to iron my clothes and my dad would ask me to iron his shirts for him. My dad taught me how to shave the hair off of the back of his neck using a razor. I did my best not to nick him on his neck and cause him to bleed. Mom was determined to make all of her children self-sufficient when we grew up. My father cut my brothers' hair and my brothers learned how to cut hair from watching my dad. He was a jack-of-all-trades and the disciplinarian in the family.

If we got in trouble at school, dad would go to the school and whip us in front of our classmates. You did not want to mess with my dad (aka Duke). My parents punished us when we did wrong. They whipped us with a switch, belt, or by hand, whichever one they could get to first. The ironic thing about it was we had to go outside and pick our own switch from the tree in our front yard. I can tell you right now, you don't know how many times my brothers and I wanted to cut that tree down! The whippings never killed or injured us; even though we had whelps on our legs or backs, the swelling went down and we were fine. Trust me, we got the message and we turned out to be disciplined children and we never got in any major trouble growing up. The Bible says, "If you spare the rod, you spoil the child." My dad put the fear of God in us and I thank him because it kept me out of trouble. My dad served in the United States Army for four years. He was a man of many trades and talents. He had a personalized book of matches made with his black and white glossy picture on the front cover. Dad was brilliant and always did amazing things that impressed and encouraged me. I have a lot of things in common with my dad. He was the handyman around the house and repaired everything from electrical problems to plumbing issues.

Every Friday we had the traditional fish dinner. It was a religious ritual that mom and the neighbors celebrated, Good Friday, the day that Jesus was crucified. There were lots of Christians and believers in my neighborhood. Our Sunday dinner was always our best dinner of the week. My mom made homemade rolls for dinner. The aroma from the smell of the yeast made the house smell like a bakery. We couldn't wait for mom to put the pans of rolls in the oven to bake so we could stuff them in our mouth and eat them. My mom was a good cook; she even made homemade hoecakes and biscuits from scratch.

My brothers and I never had birthday parties, but Mom made sure that all of us celebrated our birthday with cake and ice cream. Mom always made each of us a birthday cake, and when she was mixing the cake batter in the bowl, we would ask if we could lick the spoon. The cakes were fluffy and decorated with our favorite frosting and lit candles. The family would gather around the dinner table and dim the lights and sing the happy birthday song. Our birthday gifts were usually comic books, socks, coloring books, puzzles, toys, or a few dollars in a card. Comic books were very popular and affordable. We found Superman, Batman, the Green Hornet, Wonder Woman, and other superheroes entertaining.

We lived normal lives. Mom helped us with our homework and attended the PTA meetings at our school. At night, she tucked us in and read us a bedtime story, but before going to sleep she made us pray. Mom taught us how to bend our knees, bow our heads, fold our hands, closes our eyes, and pray. She even taught us the Lord's Prayer so we wouldn't have to think about what we should pray about. My mom was the most important person in my life.

It was never my parent' intention to live and raise us in the projects forever. Thank God they eventually got better and higher paying jobs. They were able to save enough money to buy a new house on the other side of town. Mom went house hunting and found a three-story colonial row house that had everything she wanted in a house. It had three bedrooms, a living room, a kitchen, a dining room, a basement, and a front and back yard. The house was centrally located in the northeast section of the city and it was a good, safe neighborhood to raise a family.

The elementary school was a block down the street from the house. The shopping area for food, clothes and other essentials including the church and the bank were down the street within walking distance. None of us six siblings ever lived in the home at the same time. My oldest brother Jamie went into the United States Air Force right after he graduated from high school. My two younger brothers were not even born when he left home. Since I was the only girl in the family, my mom and I would sit and talk about girly things like my menstrual period and other things. I clearly remember when she sat me down one day and said, "Linda, don't depend on a man or anyone for anything; work hard and get whatever you need and want for yourself." Her conversation resonated with me over the years even to this day, and I had no problem working for the things that I needed and wanted.

I got my first job when I was 14 years old. I worked after school at a daycare school in our neighborhood. My youngest two brothers went to that daycare. I worked full time in the summer when school was out. The owner of the daycare was a white lady who weighed 300 lbs. and got around very slowly. She had long hair down to her butt and it was my job to comb her hair for her. Sometimes I had to help her take a bath. She was one of the nicest people you could every meet. I learned a lot about daycare while working for her and I loved her.

When I started high school, I got a part time job working in the evenings for the United Planning Organization (UPO). In the summer I worked full time. The principal at my high school announced over the PA system that a client was looking for a student to come to her house to iron clothes on a part-time basis. Even though I couldn't make the clothes look like they came from the cleaners, I ironed the clothes well enough to get the wrinkles out and the client never complained. At the age of 16, that money came in handy. I was able to buy things to start a hope chest and save those things for my marriage. Back in the day most girls started a hope chest. My brothers had ways of making money for themselves. Two of my brothers had paper routes and two of my brothers worked with my father at the baseball stadium selling hotdogs, popcorn, and peanuts. All of us learned how to make money when we were growing up.

My uncle Maury Wills, my father's younger brother always played baseball. When Maury was playing ball at a baseball clinic in Parkside, a black neighborhood, in Kenilworth, he and his friends noticed a white man, Gerry Priddy, watching the game for several hours. Mr. Priddy was the coach for he all-white Washington Senators Major League Baseball Team. Maury was a fast runner; he ran like he had wings on the bottom of his feet. He was stealing bases without getting caught and that impressed Mr. Priddy. Maury's defensive performance on the field also stood out. Mr. Priddy sat with the team and talked with them for hours. It was that blessed day when he recruited Maury to play professional baseball. Maury soon moved to Spokane, Washington, with his family to attend training camp. He played his first major league game in 1951 for the Los Angeles Dodgers.

The Wills' family and friends watched the Dodgers games on television whenever Maury played. The businesses in the area were calling my grandparents' home looking for one of my aunts or uncles to represent their companies' product. The Johnson Business School hired my aunt Betty, Maury's youngest sister, to do a radio commercial for them to advertise the Johnson Business School and to mention in the commercial that she was Maury's sister. At that time aunt Betty was a student herself at Eastern High School. Maury was named the Most Valuable Player (MVP) in 1962. He became a spokesman on NBC Sports *Game of the Week* that broadcasted every Saturday on television. In 2011, the Banneker Field on Georgia Avenue in D.C. was renamed "The Maury Wills Field." The field was dedicated to Maury for his contribution to baseball and for representing his hometown, Washington, D.C. Mayor Adrian Fenty and the city council took part in the groundbreaking ceremony that day. To this day, Maury runs a baseball clinic every summer at the Banneker Field for the youth in DC who are interested in playing baseball. The Mayor's office hosted a reception for Maury at the Wilson building and presented him with a proclamation and the Key to the City.

# Chapter Two

## Tragedies – from JFK to MLK— That Affected my Life

In 1963 when the news was broadcasted that President John F. Kennedy was assassinated, I was just a young girl. When I saw the look of hurt on my mom's face, I was devastated because she started to cry. My mom had a lot of respect for President John F. Kennedy because he cared about the concerns of the black community and he did what he could as the President of the United States to soften the blows for African American citizens. My mom took us to the Capitol building to see the President's casket lying in state. We stood in line outside for hours, in the cold with thousands of people, waiting to go into the Capitol building to pay homage to our slain President. The public viewing lasted for a couple of days. His casket was draped with the American flag and guarded by the military's best. I grieved his death for many years. It was hard for me to believe that someone had killed the President--now we people of color would have to start all over again with a new President who may not have the same passion for the African American people as President John F. Kennedy had. My people of color had hope in the system, but the enemy was always plotting to get rid of anyone who upheld the black struggle.

In 1968 Martin Luther King was assassinated. Riots started breaking out across the country. As I was leaving work, a white man who was extremely afraid to leave the building asked me if he could leave out with me. To my knowledge, no one was safe that day. I rushed to the bus stop and boarded the bus for home. When the bus driver pulled into the downtown area, I saw a group of men attempting to break into a jewelry store. When the bus driver pulled onto my block, I jumped off the bus and ran across the street into my house. I could smell smoke in the air coming from the burning buildings on 8th Street. The screeching sound of the fire engines could be heard from a distance.

My mom told my brothers not to go down on 8th Street. I had to get a closer look to see what was really going on so I ran down the street to get a closer look. The smell and cloud of smoke got in my eyes, nose and throat making it difficult for me to see or breathe. The massive crowd of people in the streets just didn't seem real, not in my neighborhood. Some of the people who came from out of nowhere were breaking into the stores and stealing televisions, appliances, clothes, and other goods. The crowds were running from one side of the street to the other; it was total chaos and I didn't see a police man in sight.

The city government had to call a city curfew and the youth had to be indoors and off of the streets by 9:00 p.m. My mom would let my younger brothers sit out front on the porch with her during the curfew hours when she was off of work. For me it was such a tragedy to see the country in such a turmoil. Racism is built into the fabric of this country in my opinion, and it still exists in the year 2015.

Dr. Martin Luther King, Jr. was a civil rights leader who stood for justice and peace for all people. He was paving the way for African Americans to have the same civil rights that white Americans enjoyed. I have marched in Memphis, TN to Washington, DC for the things that he stood for. His assassination came with a heavy price, to this country, and by the same token we, African Americans got some affirmation when James Brown released "Say It Loud, I'm Black and I'm Proud." We loved that song and the black radio stations turned it into an anthem, and they played it in heavy rotation, forever it seemed. The Black Panther Party, the Southern Christian Leadership Conference (chaired by Dr. King before he was assassinated), and other black power groups soon led an enormous movement in this country. The ruins and scars from the riots in 1963 remained visible for more than twenty years, in Washington, DC and other cities across the nation. As a native I have looked at the ruins year in and year out for over twenty years.

In the 1972 the Watergate Hotel Scandal led to the impeachment of President Richard M. Nixon, from the Office of President of the United States. An African-American security guard discovered a break in at the Democratic National Committee Headquarters at the Watergate Office Complex in Washington, D.C. and reported it to his superiors. Some of the men caught in the break-in were the President's men and the Nixon administration attempted to cover-up his involvement. It was the greatest political scandal in the history of this country. My family along with everyone else in the country watched the trial play out on national television. President Richard Nixon (a.k.a. Tricky Dick) and his men were found guilty of the break in. Nixon, a Republican was impeached from the Office of the President of the United States. The young black man who reported the break in was allegedly fired from his job. I say shame on you, whoever you are, for firing him instead of making him what he was: a national hero. That kind of behavior (the firing of that young man) left me and many other African Americans feeling unprotected and disrespected.

# CHAPTER THREE

## Inner City Living

The city had a Human Kindness Day. It was a weekend celebration for the people in this city that took place on the waterfront in S.W. More than 100,000 people turned out for the celebration. There were plenty of food, drinks, festivities, speakers, and loads of fun. It was in the heart of the summer and people wore shorts, straw hats and flip-flops. Some had picnic baskets full of food and drinks. They sat around the Tidal Basin (Haines Point) until the park was closed each day. This was the baby boomer, liberated hippy generation living it up, and transitioning into a new era and a new way of living.

In 1977 there was a huge marijuana smoke-out for the legalization of pot held in Lafayette Park near the White House. Thousands of people attended the rally and smoked pot in the park all day. This was the Age of Aquarius in the 1960's and 1970's. A May Day protest against the Vietnam War was held on the National Mall and hundreds of thousands of people flooded the mall that day to protest the Vietnam War. The Harikrishnans, from the country of India, had a major presence in Washington D.C. for many years. They were visible in the airports, train stations, bus stations, and downtown and on major street corners in the city. They sold incense and other products; sometimes you could see and hear them chant. The women were dressed in Sari dresses, and the men were dressed in the Dholi and Kurta their native dress, with sandal shoes. The African Americans wore big bush hairstyles and dashikis.

Many African American Washingtonians made major contributions to the Nation's Capitol. Robert D. Hooks (actor) and Douglas Turner Ward founded the Negro Ensemble Company in Washington, DC. Joseph Wilson and Maurice McIntosh owned a car dealership in the city, and everyone bought cars from that dealership. Sharon Pratt Kelly was the first African American and first female mayor of Washington, DC. Two sisters who could pass for white owned Cecilia's Restaurant. It was in a great location across the street from the Howard Theatre and it was a popular eating-place. Most of the entertainers who performed at the Howard dined at Cecilia's. My friend Melvin Lindsey, at WHUR radio station started the *"The Quiet Storm"* radio show, and it became one of the top radio shows in the city. Melvin had a knack for playing the best slow jams. I could listen to Melvin on the air all night. One day I told him that I had to kiss him. LOL! He just smiled with his beautiful smile and kissed me softly. I wandered from club to club dancing back in the day. By the time I became a record promoter I knew which clubs to take my records to and who the deejays were. I went to the Coco Club, Black Tahiti, French Connection, Mark IV, RSVP, Pisces, Tiffany, Mr. Henry's, W.H. Bone, Mingles, and other clubs where professionals congregated. Sometimes, I caught a bus to U Street NW, which was a major hot spot for African American businesses. Black folks owned all types of successful businesses (law firms, accounting firms, dentist offices, construction firms, etc.) My aunt Edith owned a custard shop and my father worked as a contractor.

WOL radio station was the top black owned radio station in the city, managed by Dewey and Cathy Hughes. The urban station featured R&B music, talk and the news. Station played the music that everyone wanted to hear. Cathy was one of the DJ's on the air and she became a strong personality and was loved by many. Bobby Bennett, Her popularity soared in the District of Columbia. The television stations went off the air around midnight in those days, and came back on the air at 6 am. We only had four (4) television channels back then to watch (chl 4, 5, 7, 9). Anyone who was up after midnight was entertained by the music on the radio.

Petey Greene, a radio and television talk show host (WOL radio/ WDCA channel 20 television) offered me an opportunity to co-host, with him, his television show. Petey had a radio show called "Rapping with Petey Greene" and his television show Petey Greene's Washington, won several Emmy awards. Petey was invited by Jimmy Carter to visit the White House. It was quite an experience, and astonishing time for me to be extended the opportunity to co-host Petey's television show. He mentored and showed me how to co-host and interview the guest. We interviewed Ed Murphy, a prominent citizen and African- American business leader, in the city (DC). Ed was in the process of building the Harambee House hotel, the first African American operated and owned hotel in the United States. He showed us the clay model of the hotel and the blueprints. The hotel diagram featured 150-room luxury rooms, full service amenities; swimming pool, health spa, coffee shop, bars, lounges, supper club, ballroom, banquet/meeting rooms, luxury suites, saunas; beauty and barber shops, a boutique and indoor parking. They broke ground, for the hotel, across the street from the campus of Howard University, and adjacent to Ed Murphy's Supper Club, on Georgia Avenue, NW, Washington, DC. I was honored to be a part of history in the making. Murph, his close friends called him, and I became close friends and colleagues. When the luxury hotel was built, it was patronized by politicians, celebrities in the music and entertainment industry as well as the students at Howard and the general public.

When I returned home, to Washington, DC, after working on the road in the music industry for many years, I was offered a partnership, by the owners of Galaxy Unlimited Records, a local recording company based in Washington, DC, to become a partner in the company. I was a hometown girl, who dated and worked for singer Al Green and my peers started calling me their hometown celebrity. I had a wealth of knowledge about the entertainment industry, and I made lots of friends and contacts along the way. Galaxy Unlimited was owned by three guys Charlie Moreland, Esquire, Charles Stevenson, an assistant to Congress Ronald Dellum and Bruce Bennett, son to a professor at Hampton University. It was three groups signed to the label at that time, Experience Unlimited (EU) Sugar Bear's go-go group; Lerene Flack, sister to Roberta Flack, an R&B artist, and Black Sheep a Reggae band who was awesome. I took the experience and knowledge that I learned working for Al and used it to help move the company forward. We never had a problem, getting our records played on the radio in the DC market and each group/artist performed a lot in the DMV (DC, MD, VA). Galaxy Unlimited Records was also an independent contractor for one of the major record labels.

I was walking down the street on a cool September day in 1976 and I met a man name Mr. H. Wilson. We began to talk and eventually over a period of time we became friends. He was a socialite and a businessman who was involved in politics. Mr. Wilson lived on the gold coast in DC and was known for hosting some of the best soirees in town. If you didn't know him you had to know someone who knew him in order for you to get into his parties. He introduced me to Marion Barry his good friend and colleague. He also had some affiliations with the record industry. He offered me an opportunity to be on the album cover for one of his projects. He was going to photograph me in nude and use the picture as a silhouette for the cover, but I turned down the offer. I was attending a fundraiser for Mayor Marion Barry and was approached by a wealthy, good looking Caucasian man. He couldn't keep his eyes off of me or my bowlegs so he started a conversation with me. He was a big supporter of Marion Barry. We became friends and started dating after knowing each other for months. He gave me a job working for his company and things were good for me for a while. One day he asks me if I wanted to start my own business. He was going to front the money, the building and the equipment to start a data processing company. By all means it would have been his business and I would have been the front person. I reluctantly turn down the offer because I did not have any experience in that area and I didn't want to run the risk of ruining his business. I eventually ended the relationship when I found out that he was married. I didn't feel good about dating a married man. I was not brought up to be a home wrecker or adulteress; my conscious wouldn't allow me to continue in the relationship, I didn't want the bad coma so the relationship ended.

Prior to those beautiful years, my parents encouraged me and my brothers to attend vocational schools after we graduated from junior high. My parents could not afford to send us to college. My brother Cornell studied masonry at Armstrong vocational school and received his certification in masonry. I attended a vocational high school and studied secretarial training. As a part of the course, I had to take a test at the Civil Service Commission (CSC), and pass the test before I could complete the course and graduate. Several weeks after taking and passing the test, I received a letter from the federal government offering me a job as a clerk-stenographer. Learning the trade, Secretarial Training, landed me a job years later, working for singer, Al Green as his Personal Secretary. The city promoted vocational schools (MM Washington, Phelps, Bell, Chamberlain and Bell) and a number of them were spread though out the city. MM Washington was name after George Washington's wife Betsy. The school offered tailoring, home economics, nursing, cosmetology, dressmaking and food services courses. The academic classes that I told were: Science, English, Math, Social Studies, and Chemistry, not to mention gym and drivers education. I enjoyed shorthand and typing. The city was waiting to bring people into the workforce that graduated from vocational schools. The level of training and experience from those schools was sufficient for the workplace.

After being exposed to and working with people in the political arena, I was encouraged to take on more leadership roles and serve in my community. I organized a cleanup campaign on my block in the neighborhood. My young neighbors and I would get up early Saturday morning and clean the streets and sidewalks, on our block. I lived on a street that had a bus stop on all four corners and the bus routes were going in four different directions (northeast, southeast, northwest and southwest). The people who waited at those bus stops morning, noon, evening and night would litter leaving our community trashy and unsanitary. After we finished cleaning the area I grilled food in my backyard and we ate hotdogs, hamburgers, potato chips, and soft drinks. That was all that I had to offer my volunteers for doing the work. When the word about my cleanup campaign got back to the City Council's office I was paid a visit by Mr. McCall, from Council John Wilson's office about the great work that I was doing in the community. After holding an extensive conversation with him he asks me if I wanted to go back to college and get my degree because I told him that I attended Federal City College, but dropped out after I became pregnant. He made arrangements with Council Wilson's office, to get me a grant to attend American University (AU).

I have worked in many political campaigns. I taught tap dancing to the young girls on my block, donated nearly one gallon of blood to the American Red Cross, and donated lots of money to charities to support the less fortunate. I support the Tom Joyner cruise each year because part of the proceeds, from the cruise, goes toward the Historical Black Colleges and Universities (HBCUs) to support our youth who are in college by way of giving them scholarships. I would be remiss if I didn't tell you how much fun I have on the cruise in addition to supporting a worthy cause.

In 1981 when I was a student at AU, interning at WKYS radio station, I met Stevie Wonder. One of my co-workers, Charlie, was working as a bodyguard for Stevie and he introduced us. Stevie and I became good friends. Stevie never really called me by my name; he called me the Capricorn and I called him, Steve land. One day when we were playing around in the hotel room, Charlie decided to hide Stevie in a big chest in the hotel room and told everyone that he couldn't find Stevie. To the three of us it was funny, but to his brother Calvin and security John and Billy it wasn't so funny. Stevie loved to joke and play around. Stevie wanted to know what I was doing at WKYS radio station because he had a radio station in LA and a company called Black Bull Productions. I would have loved to work for Stevie at his radio station in LA, but I was just learning the operation of the music department at WKYS in Washington, DC and I was still attending college.

Stevie prepared everyone in the country to celebrate Dr. Martin L. King's birthday by singing the "Happy Birthday" song that he wrote in honor of Dr. King's birthday. The song was phenomenal and slowly but surely African Americans replaced the traditional happy birthday song with Stevie's version of happy birthday. In 1982 on the day of the big march on Washington, DC to make Dr. King's birthday a national holiday, the city saw inclement weather. Nevertheless, the people kept coming despite the weather conditions. When Stevie and the rest of us arrived on the scene and Stevie got out of the limousine, the rain immediately stopped. At that moment, I knew that God was in the mix supporting the march and all of Stevie's hard work and dedication to make Dr. King's birthday a national holiday. We marched down Pennsylvania in a crowd of no less than 100,000 people. The following year, President Ronald Regan signed into law a national holiday, honoring Dr. Martin L. King's birthday so in the second to third week of every January, the nation celebrates his birthday. Watching and studying Stevie's methods and ways of dealing with political issues inspired me to challenge myself with my life goals.

Mrs. Lorie Murray, a community activist in my neighborhood, asked me to run for the Advisory Neighborhood Commissioner (ANC) seat for Ward 2C16 in 1986, but I declined the position. I wasn't interested in politics to that extent, but Mrs. Murray talked me into it. Washington, DC is split by single member districts (SMD) of 2,000 people and the registered voters in those wards vote on Election Day for the ANC. I didn't think I could get enough voters to vote for me but Mrs. Murray campaigned for me and I won the election as the ANC to serve a two-year term. I dealt with issues ranging from sanitation, police protection, health, education and other things that affect the wellbeing of the people. At the end of my term, the mayor's office (Marion Barry's Administration) awarded me with a certificate of appreciation for my work and tenure at the ANC. Since that time I've worked on other local/political campaigns. I worked on former Congressman Walter Fauntroy's campaign many years ago, former President Bill Clinton and President Barack Obama's campaign.

I have had so many opportunities to do so many different things in my life. I joined the Precola DeVore Charm and Modeling School, in Washington, DC in the 1980's. I was fortunate enough to be chosen by Mrs. DeVore to be one of the ringside girls in ring at a professional boxing match. I walked around in the ring holding up the round cards, at the George Foreman–Ken Norton fight at the DC Armory. My modeling life span was short because I wanted to be a runway model, but I was too short. However, I did qualify for print media, but I wanted the runway and didn't pursue a career in modeling.

In the year 2000, I applied for a job as a flight attendant at Trans States Airlines (TSA) and was given an opportunity to try out for the position. TSA was a small independent airline that did contract work for the major airlines. After I completed training I was flying for the airlines 6 days a week. We flew short distance flights on the east coast for the majors. I learned how to manage people, how to give CPR and first aid; how to institute safety measures, and everything about a fuselage. I enjoyed working with the pilots, first officers and talking to the passengers over the PA system giving safety instructions and training. The Federal Aviation Administration inspectors inspected the airplanes at every stop for mechanical problems. Sometimes our planes were taken out of the fleet, for mechanical reasons. One day while we were in flight, the plane dropped 500 feet suddenly and caught me off guard, and I screamed. I left the airlines and got a job working on land months later.

On September 11, 2001, when I arrived at work, the office staff was in the bosses' office with their eyes glued watching the television. Richard, my supervisor told me with a weird sense of excitement to watch the television. As I started to watch, I saw the two airplanes crash into the twin towers of the World Trade Center. I felt sad and fearful for the people who were trapped in the towers. I was overcome with fright for my own life at that point. Minutes later a plane crashed into one of the buildings at the Pentagon in Virginia and burst into flames. I could not believe my eyes and had to wipe them several times to make sure that my eyes were not playing tricks on me. Everything was surreal. I decided at that moment that it would be best for me if I left work and went home. I ran into my manager's office and told him that the Pentagon was hit and that I was leaving work. The news reporter said that there was a plane circling in Pennsylvania headed for the U.S. Capitol Building in Washington, DC. The US Capitol was a stone's throw away from the building where I was working and I wasn't taking any chances of being in the area if the plane was headed our way. When I left the building and went outside there were people already crowded in the streets running, crying, trying to make calls on their cell phones. It was shear panic everywhere and the gridlock in the street from the cars, trucks, and buses caused a massive traffic jam. As I was walking home, I tried to call my mom, but my cell phone wasn't working. The bandwidth couldn't handle the volume of calls. I watched the news for the rest of the day and night; I was too afraid to go to sleep.

# CHAPTER FOUR

## My Greatest Losses

I moved my 14 year old son James to California to live with my brother Everett and his family, to protect him from living a thug life. Everett was a United States Marine and lived on the military base in Treasure Island, outside of San Francisco California. He and his wife April were known for taking in family members in the time of need. The nice neighborhood that we lived in suddenly became a crime zone (a drug haven for dealers and users. People were known to have traveled from as far away as the state of Pennsylvania to our neighborhood to buy drugs (cocaine). James enjoyed living on the military base; he played on the baseball team with the soldiers and was one of their star players. James was very good at sports; I guess it ran in our family.

After Everett completed his tour in California, he spent the remainder of his time in service in Alameda, Georgia. In Alameda, James attended the predominately white Osborne High School. He joined the basketball team and became the star player for the team that went from last place to first place in the high schools competition. James was named the Most Valuable Player (MVP) for the 1988 – 1989 seasons at Osborne High. After he graduated he wanted to come home instead of going straight to college. Our neighborhood was still a breeding and training ground for drug traffickers. After being home for a couple of years, he became a victim of gun violence and was shot and killed in the neighborhood. At that point, my whole world fell apart I didn't want to live any longer. I got a phone call from the eye bank hours after my son died who were asking me if I would donate his eyes.

I began to travel the streets in the neighborhood day and night asking questions and trying to find the person who killed my son. As far as I was concerned, it was going to be an eye for an eye. His friends and family members were on the lookout as well, searching for the killer to bring him or them to justice—street justice.

My father died a year after my son died in 1992 from a heart attack; he was 66 years old. In 1993 my brother Cornell died from pneumonia and he was only 46 years old. In 1994 my 96 year old grandmother died; she was the mid-wife who delivered me when I was born. In 1995, my mom's only sibling Patricia died from a heart attack. In 1996, my uncle Jack died of a heart attack at the age of 75 years old. My brother Everett said, "Death ain't a stranger in our house." Finally things slowed down, but in 2007 my oldest brother Jamie died from heart complications.

In July 2005, my mom called me and told me that she couldn't breathe, and that she was stuck on the stairs in the house. I got in my car and raced over to her house to rescue her. When I saw my mom standing on the stairs I ran upstairs to help her back to her bedroom until the ambulance arrived. I raced over to the neighbor's house and told her to call the ambulance. When they arrived the paramedics arrived they asked a bunch of questions. I told them to get her to Washington Hospital Center as fast as they could. While we were in the ambulance one of the paramedics called ahead to the emergency room to let them know that they had a heart patient on the way. The hospital told the paramedic that the emergency room was full and they couldn't take any more patients at that time. The next closest hospital was Howard University Hospital (HUH). We had no choice but to go there. The doctor in the emergency room discovered four leaking heart valves in Mom's heart. The fluid was leaking into her lungs making her short of breath. Mom was too old for heart surgery at the age of 87, so the doctor did patch work essentially to slow the leaking.

I arranged for a heart and geriatrics doctor to monitor her symptoms and exam her on a regular basis, before and after she was hospitalized. I was counting on both of them to keep my mom alive! After she was strong enough to come home from the hospital, we hired a home nurse to come to the house and care for her when we were at work. My nephew Gambriel really loved Mom and he came to the house every Thursday to spend time with her, and he called her during the week just to check on her. They watched the *Wheel of Fortune* together, one of her favorite television shows. Mom knew the answers to most of the puzzles before the actual contestants. Mom would have won a lot of money on the show had she been a contestant. Gabriel contributed money towards the nurse assistant's salary that we paid weekly.

My mom had an allergic reaction to one of her medications and I had to put her in my car and rush her to the emergency room at the hospital. While she was lying on the hospital bed, she reached up with her hand and held my chin and said, "Don't be scared." She was concerned about me instead of thinking of herself. That was an amazing moment in my life, her unconditional love that she had for me was unspeakable. She has always demonstrated and showed us lots of love.

In 2011 after mom regained some of her strength I took her on a White House tour. It was something she had always wanted to do. I wheeled her around in a wheelchair because she was too weak and in too much pain to walk. When the tour guide saw me struggling with her in the wheelchair and the look of pain that showed in her face, he took us on the elevator to the downstairs level. He gave us a mini tour and showed us the kitchen where the chefs prepare the meals for the first family. He pointed out an area where part of the kitchen caught on fire (wood over the ceiling) that was done by the British when they tried to burn the White House down in the 1800s. Mom attended many events with me before she died.

When I was the keynote speaker at an event hosted by Margaret Dureke, the President of Women Empowered to Achieve the Impossible (WETATI), my mom attended the event even though she was in a lot of pain. Mom lived vicariously through me, as well as others, at times. I did a lot of things that she herself, had a desire to do, but never had the opportunity.

The Christmas before mom died, she was in the hospital, too sick to come home. Every year the family—siblings, grandchildren, great-grandchildren, cousins, nieces, nephews, and in-laws—had a pot luck Christmas dinner at her house to celebrate the birth of Christ and to exchange gifts with each other. We were considering spending Christmas day with mom in the hospital and cancelling the dinner, but she told us to go on with the tradition and have Christmas dinner with the family without her. Mom was always putting us first; she didn't have a selfish bone in her body especially when it came to her family.

When Mom died my brothers and I prepared the program and handled all of the arrangements for her home going celebration at the Pilgrim Baptist Church. The church was full from the front door to the main fellowship hall, to the balcony with friends and family. The people came to pay their respects. Jeff Holden, of the group the Holden Brothers, sang "Troubles of the World" and Al Johnson, sang his hit record, "The 23 Psalm" and turned the church out. Both artists contributed their angelic voices, in song, as a tribute to mom, and as a favor to me. They were my friends and colleagues in the record industry.

My brother Melvin, Doctor and Bishop officiated over the funeral. I wrote a poem a poem about Mom called the "Virtuous Woman" and it read like this: "Mom you were the pillar of strength that kept our family together like a bird brooding over her nest through all types of weather. You protected us through thick and thin and your words of wisdom always sunk in. The virtuous woman you were, your character, your posture, and your Christian ways hung around your neck all through your days. God used you as a vessel of hope, never fearing, always caring and big on sharing. As the light in the lighthouse with your soft-spoken voice, you always made for your family the right choice. And yes, you always seemed to stand out in the crowd. You were sweet and gentle and we were so proud of you. Being the children of an angel sent from above, you showered everyone you met with your love. So as the night moved on and we left your side, the Holy Spirit sent his angels to be by your side, to get you ready for the pearly gates, to sit with the Lord in his heavenly grace."

My brother Everett, Gunnery Sergeant, formerly of the U.S. Marines, and brother Mark, Pastor of Change of Heart Ministries, gave various reflections. Others spoke and Pastor Jones gave beautiful words of reverence about mom. He adored her as one of the mothers of the church that he admired and she accepted him as her Pastor. The music ministry, under the leadership of Christopher Jon, went forth with songs of Zion. The ushers, choir members, and other people participated in the service and repast. Now that I have given you some memoirs about my life growing up as an African American in the Nation's Capital, please let me tell you about my amazing love affair with a superstar and how I got involved in the record industry.

# PART TWO

## LIFE WITH A SUPERSTAR

# Chapter Five

## My Amazing Love Affair

One of my favorite songs in 1972 was "I'm Tired of Being Alone" by Al Green. That song spoke to my life and was telling my story. I fell in love with Al Green through his music. When it was announced on the radio station that Al Green was coming to Washington D.C. to do a show at the Loebs Palace Theatre, I asked my friends Katrina and Carol to go with me to the show. Al had become my imaginary lover and I wanted to see and hear him sing my favorite song, "I'm Tired of Being Alone." I even wanted to catch the sweat from his brow. We had front row seats; it couldn't get any better than that I thought.

After the show, while my friends and I stood out front of the theatre and reminisced, all of a sudden the doors of the bus that was parked in front of the theatre swung open and a six-foot eight inch tall man stepped off of the bus and he walked over to us. He said, "Hi, my name is Oliver Ingram, and I work for Al Green as his valet and bodyguard." He asked if we wanted to see the bus, so we said yes ok, but we were puzzled that he wanted to show off Al's bus. Before getting off of the bus, Oliver asked if we wanted to meet Al Green. "Of course we do," I said and that was the highlight and turning point for that evening and even for my life. God was smiling on me that night and fulfilling my prayer request to meet Al face to face.

When Oliver took us backstage it was dark and Al was standing on the side of the stage by himself. When I laid my eyes on him I was all in from there. I was asking myself is this really real? Oliver walked us over to Al and introduced us one by one. When he introduced me, Al leaned over and kissed me softly on my lips, then he gave me a big beautiful smile! I think he may have seen me cutting up, clowning and going nuts over him when he was on the stage performing, so he was showing his appreciation for my support. I don't know why he kissed me for real, but it sent my rocket to the moon. I began to melt like butter in a frying pan. I was excited, overwhelmed and elated. He was very handsome, friendly and spoke in a soft voice when he said hello. Before we left the theatre that night, to go home, Oliver invited us to an after-party at their hotel. As much as I wanted to I told Oliver that we couldn't make the party. I told Oliver that we would love to see them before they left town the next day.

The next day around noon I called Oliver and told him that we were on our way to see them. It was so ironic that the hotel was only blocks away from the building where we worked. Carol and I worked in the same office. I was fortunate enough to get her a job in the office working with me, and Katrina worked around the corner at a law firm. The three of us walked around the corner to the hotel. When we got there Oliver was waiting for us in front of the building. He had a crush on Katrina so he was happy to see all of us. He took us upstairs to see Al. When we got to his room, he was dragging his luggage into the hallway getting ready for check out. Thank God we got to the hotel just in time to catch him before he left. When he saw me, he walked over to speak and he greeted me with a kiss. This time, I closed my eyes and I started to French kiss him. After we were in the moment, he jumped back, laughed and said "This is a fast one!" I started to laugh at him, and then we exchanged telephone phone numbers and said we would call each other. I was dressed in a beige suede miniskirt, a cream silk blouse, knee-high beige suede boots, with a designer bag hung over my shoulder. I wanted his eyes to be focused on me and only me.

I started calling him on the WATTS line at work and from home at night. We would talk for hours, getting to know each other. Four months later, I told Al that I wanted to see him; the feeling was mutual. He finally called me and invited me to meet him in Cherry Hill, NJ. He was performing at the Latin Casino Hotel for a couple of days. New Jersey was only three hundred miles away from Washington, D.C. so Carol and I drove up on a beautiful warm summer day in 1972. It felt like magic was all around me and it was one of the happiest days of my life. When we arrived at the hotel, Oliver was in the lobby waiting for me. I checked in at the front desk and gave Oliver my room number to give to Al. He was at sound check preparing for his show for that night. After Carol and I got dressed for the show later on in the evening, we went downstairs to the front lobby of the hotel where Roland, Al's road manager, was waiting to escort us to the Latin Casino. When we got there, Roland seated us at a table with a white table cloth in front of the stage tablecloth where Al could see me. I had on a jersey knit burgundy two piece suit with a fitting wraparound skirt that fit my body like a custom-made piece. My burgundy suede clogs completed the look.

Al put on a stunning show that night. He handed me a beautiful red rose. After the show was over, I went back to my hotel room and I waited, with abated breath for Al's phone call. The phone rang around midnight and it was Al calling, inviting me to come to his room. When he opened his door to let me in his room it was dimly lit. He was dressed in a pair black of silk pajamas with a smoking jacket that hung open. He smelled like a million dollars and romance filled the air immediately. It was a magical, romantic, kind of passion that submerged us. The heat of passion consumed us as we consummated our relationship. This was not a one-night affair; this was real and we wanted to take our relationship to a higher level.

When Al was booked at the Apollo Theater, in New York City for a weekend, he invited me to visit with him. This time, Katrina and I drove together in her brand new Camaro. Oliver was glad because he wanted to see Katrina and they were hitting it off. The trip turned into a journey for me instead of a weekend visit. I was supposed to have stayed in New York until Sunday, but instead, it turned into a four-and-a-half-day trip. Katrina had to leave early Sunday morning. She and Oliver never really got together because she had a boyfriend. When I told Al that I was leaving too, he told me to stay with him and that he would see to it that I got back home safely, so I stayed with him for a couple of more days. On Monday morning, I traveled with Al and the Enterprise Band, in his Silver Eagle tour bus, to Hampton, Virginia. When Wednesday rolled around, I was still with him. I called home to talk with my mom and she told me that she was sending my brother Melvin to pick me up from wherever I was to bring back me home. When my brother came to pick me up, my son's father was with him. This created some drama but for a short time because I was now in love with Al and he was the only man that I wanted in my life. As time went on, I wanted to spend more time with Al. The lovemaking between us was supernatural and I wanted more of him.

As usual, we are again talking on the phone to each other, in the wee hours of the morning (3:00 am), and I broke the female code and told him that I was in love with him. When I asked how he felt about me he said, "I feel good about you." He then said, "Girl don't you know that it is 3:00 in the morning?" and I said, "yes." As the conversation continued, he invited me to Memphis that day to visit with him. He gave me instructions on what to do when I arrived at the airport, so I booked a flight on Braniff Airlines and went to Memphis.

When I arrived in Memphis, I took a cab to his place and was greeted by his secretary who was working in his office. When Al arrived at the house later, he gently kissed me with his butter-soft full lips and the shock waves shot through my entire body. We went out to dinner that night at the Four Flames Restaurant. After dinner, we went to Hi Recording Studio. Willie Mitchell owned Hi Records and was an affiliate of London Records. Willie was the person who discovered Al in a club out of town. That night I met Willie, the Hodges Brothers and his other studio musicians.

Al went into the recording booth and started to sing, "Something's going on, someone's on the phone 3:00 o'clock in the morning, talking 'bout how she can make it right. Love is when you really feel good about somebody, ain't nothing wrong being in love with someone oh baby: Love and Happiness." As I sat there and listened to the lyrics to the song, I realized that he wrote the song about our love affair and phone conversation that we had earlier that morning. Wow, I couldn't imagine the beauty of our love was captured in a song. I thought to myself, "Is this really real, or am I dreaming?" It was an amazing feeling for me to know that I inspired happiness in Al's life. That night we made love like Romeo and Juliet, and it was freaking fantastic. When he put the record out, the radio stations put it in a heavy rotation and 35 years later they are still playing our song. The general public went nuts over the song, and it became a hit record. Our affair became richer, stronger, and more purposeful. It was a fairy-tale romance; I felt like Cinderella and my life was hanging in the balance depending on God to see Al and I through thick and thin.

One cold October day, when I was in the house chilling with my brother Cornell, Al called me on the phone with some exciting news. He said that he wanted to talk to me about working for him and he offered me a job as his personal secretary. I told him to hold on for a minute and turned to my brother with excitement and told him about the job offer. He immediately said, "Charge him five hundred dollars a week." For me, Al's timing was perfect. I needed a change of life for the better. I knew he was looking for a replacement for his secretary, who traveled with him, but I didn't think that it would be me who he had in mind for the position. I already had a job working in the Federal government as a secretary. I was on a detail to Benjamin J. Hooks, the first African-American Commissioner at the FCC's office. I was working for him until his executive assistant arrived in town from Memphis, Tennessee. When Al offered me the job, I knew that I was perfect for the position, but I didn't know if my parents were going to support me and take care of my son James while I was away. My office gave me a going away party and wished me well. I resigned from the Commission after working there for 5 years. Weeks later, I packed my clothes and Cornell drove me to Baltimore to meet up with Al and the Enterprise Band. Only God could have made something so wonderful happen to me. He honored my prayer to remove me out of an abusive relationship with my son's father who was dating me and other women and having babies by all of us, and he turned out to be a married man who cheated on his wife and each of the women he was dating. I prayed so hard to God to remove that stumbling block from my path so I could get a life and breathe again.

Hallelujah, God did more than move me from a bad situation, he moved me out of town. The scripture says that God will give you beauty for your ashes, and that is exactly what he had done for me. He turned my life around 360 degrees. I knew that I had an arduous task ahead of me working for Al in the entertainment industry, but I knew that I would prevail. I was more than willing to learn the job quickly and was confident in my ability to do the administrative part of the job and to make the man that I was in love with proud of me.

# CHAPTER SIX

## Working for Green Enterprises

When I arrived at the Biltmore hotel, I called Al from the front lobby and told him that I was reporting to work. We left Baltimore the next day on his tour bus and drove to Jamaica, New York. I was responsible for handling million-dollar contracts, payroll, receipts, bank statements, and other documents; there was no room for error. Al was a superstar with a huge support network: managers, accountant services, concert promoters, record executives, staff, fans, colleagues, investors and other people were involved in this career and life. The road life is unforgiving at times and if you stay out on the road too long, it will take its toll on your body.

Living in and out of a suitcase is what I did for several years and losing luggage along the way. My position as Al's personal secretary came with lots of expectations from others. I was the go to person for him on the road and I was expected to perform no matter what the situation called for. We traveled 70% of the year, by airplane or by bus. Oliver was a good friend to me because he introduced me to Al, and he was a lot of fun to work with. The three of us with the bodyguards traveled together. Sometimes, Al was hard to get along with, but they say artistic people are unconventional and don't always do the norm. He gave fines to the band members if they played the music too loudly on stage or if they were playing the music out of tune. They fussed, murmured and complained behind Al's back, but they couldn't do anything about it because they didn't want to get fired. Al knew a lot of people and could replace any one at a moment's notice.

There were many times when I had to count tens of thousands of dollars in cash; money that Al collected from his shows. Sometimes he was a taskmaster, and for good reasons. He had a business to run and he ran it his way. He was spot-on when it came to running his business and handling his money. He was brilliant in more ways than singing and writing. Al had a large staff with multiple layers: 4 secretaries, 9 band members, family members, bodyguards, bus drivers, accountants, and an administrative assistant. I sat in front of Al's desk and worked along with him in his private area in the office. I eventually rented an apartment, in a singles complex, across the street from the office; I was tired of living from Al's house to the Holiday Inn Central when we were off the road and back in Memphis, TN.

When we traveled from city to city we never knew what to expect. When the Hanafi Muslims attacked the Wilson Building and Washington, D.C. Council, they killed Maurice Williams, a newscaster who worked for WHUR Radio Station. Marion Barry was also shot, but he survived his injury. It was a tragic day in the District of Columbia. Cathy Hughes was working at WHUR Radio Station at the time. Al was scheduled to do an interview that morning at the station, but amidst the confusion it seemed hopeless. Everyone at the radio station was sad and confused and a lot was going on in the station. When we arrived at the radio station we didn't know what had happen. When it was time for Al to do his interview, he asked Cathy if he could talk about his new record, but she said, "No, don't you know that one of our people was shot today at the district building?" While Al seemed genuinely puzzled—I knew he felt badly and was sympathetic about the death of Maurice Williams—but he also wanted to do his interview. He was preforming in DC that night. Al did a short interview and we left the station.

Everyone loved Al, even his competition. Elton John invited Al to dinner at his place, in Beverly Hills, California in 1973. The chauffer drove us through the winding hills of Beverly Hills to Elton's location. When we arrived, Elton was there to greet us. He gave Al two beautiful Polaroid cameras, the latest model. His band members played in the swimming pool, with different colored bush wigs (red, blue, yellow, red, and orange) on their heads. Elton's manager walked over to me and placed a large white gardenia in my hair. I felt so honored and valued. The petals pressed against my hair made me feel like a queen for a day. The fragrance of the flower was beautiful. The gardenia is one of my favorite flowers. Elton's personal chef prepared a delicious dinner and we ate with Elton and his group at a huge table in the dining area of the house. Maybe it is a custom of people from England to give gifts to their guest. Like the ole saying goes, "to give is a blessing and to receive is divine." I was definitely living the rock and roll lifestyle.

Willie Mitchell, Al's producer, told him that it was time for him to write another hit song. We went to Hot Springs, Arkansas so Willie and his wife drove up in Willie's car. Me, Al and his dog drove up in Al's white Eldorado Cadillac. On the way up we stopped at a corner grocery store to buy groceries. Al asked me to cook the dinner, but little did he know that I could not cook. The hotel suite had a kitchen. I called my mom in D.C. and asked her how to cook cabbage and steak. I followed her directions, but the food lacked flavor and the steak was tough. Al gave the food to the dog and we ate junk food. The next morning, Al and I sat outside of his hotel room on the ground and he wrote and played on his acoustic guitar "You Ought to Be with Me." Al was the jealous type and didn't like me talking to the band members or any other man, unless it was about business. He was very attentive as a lover, and that was fine with me. That song was about us and we lived the song in so many ways. We were inspiring to each other. He wrote about his love affairs. Al had a beautiful smile, tender touch, very passionate and sexual. All of the girls and women wanted him but I was there with him for over two years. Nevertheless he had his stable of women.

Al didn't want the housekeepers to clean his room at the hotels. Oliver or me would clean the room and replaced fresh linen for his bed and the bathroom. He was a superstar and he carried a lot of valuables with him: contracts, money, jewelry, expensive clothes, keys, contact information, phone book, and other things of value that needed to be protected and safeguarded. It wasn't worth the risk of losing my job to trust a stranger to clean his room – and risk theft.

For breakfast, Al usually ate oatmeal, bacon, eggs, toast, and orange juice. He loves Kentucky Fried Chicken. His favorite breath mint was Sucrets. He sucked on those and drank hot tea with honey and lemon to soothe his golden throat and vocal cords.

When Al and I were in New Orleans he performed at the National Association of Television and Radio Announcers (NATRA) Convention and bought the house down. While we were there he had to pick up his Rolls Royce car that had been shipped to the United States from London, England. Al was so excited—his first Rolls Royce car. As he was driving to the hotel, in the French Quarters, the police stopped him. The officer told him that he was swerving the car in the middle of the street and asked to see his driver's license. Al reached for his license in his bag then realized that he had left it at home. The officer asked me if I had a permit and told me that I would have to drive the car. Al looked at me and said, "If you crash my car, I'm going to kill you." He didn't mean it literally. I would have felt the same way had the shoe been on the other foot. Wow, my first time driving and riding in a Rolls Royce, the car of all luxury cars! Never in my wildest dreams could I have imagined such a beautiful thing happening to me. God was always making amazing things happen for me. I am so pleased with God!

The car was a masterpiece—leather seats, wood panel, automatic windows, doors, locks and more. Later, in the evening while we were in the hotel room relaxing, Al wrote and played on his acoustic guitar, "Let's Get Married Today." I wrote a few lyrics to the song, but I didn't get any credit or royalties for the part that I wrote. Writing has always been one of my passions. Sometimes I wrote lyrics and shared them with Al for his professional opinion. Even though I loved Al I wasn't ready for marriage.

Al had an interview and show in Bakersfield, California and had to be there on time and the fastest way there was by helicopter. It was an exciting ride. Al's fan club members ordered everything he sold (t-shirts, key rings, pictures, souvenir books, etc.). The souvenir staff sold hundreds of dollars worth of product at nearly every show. Some fans put on their t-shirts right away. I had to stay up late to collect and count the money that the souvenir staff turned in from the sale of the merchandise. Al's souvenir business was a lucrative business for him. The products were made of the best quality. The t-shirts and sweatshirts were made of 100% cotton with minimum shrinkage. The pictures had vibrant colors and the paper stock was good quality and didn't tear easily. The souvenir book had 8 x 10 -size pictures and pop out posters that you could hang on the wall. The key chains and buttons were keepsakes that would last forever without tarnishing. Most of the souvenir staff was Al's family members.

I didn't always get a good night's sleep and there were no particular work hours. I made the payroll and paid the band usually at night. I was good at multitasking. Al's clothes had to be taken to and picked up from the cleaners. He was particular about how he presented himself in public. His hair was always neat, his clothes were stylish; he looked good all of the time and he strutted around like a peacock. I wore long flowing dresses and wigs, when I couldn't get to the hair salon. Al and I were professional at all times, especially when we were in the public. For us, it was business by day and loving at night when we were alone and not working. Al and the Enterprise Band had a favorite slang word, "Professional," and we tried to live up to it. We even had an Enterprise knock. If there was an *a* on the door it had to be the Enterprise knock, or we wouldn't answer the door.

Al had an accident in Wisconsin and broke his hand in several places. He was in so much pain that he had his bodyguard rush him to the hospital. The next day when the fans saw the cast and sling on his hand they wanted to know what happened. He told them he was injured going through the revolving door at the hotel. When Al did one-night (back-to-back) shows in different cities, he had to fly in the Enterprise Band. I enjoyed riding on the bus on occasion. The scenery was beautiful as we traveled from place to place. Jesse Powell (may he RIP) was the best bus driver in the world and never had an accident with the bus. Al's Silver Eagle tour bus was loaded with the state of the art equipment. It had a kitchenette, bathroom, bunk beds, lounging area, a cassette player, and other amenities.

Al was playful and enjoyed having fun and eating sweets. Sometime he would look in my purse for candy bars. He enjoyed listening to other people's music. Some of his favorite songs were "Pretty Woman" by Roy Orbison. He performed that song on stage and recorded it for one of his albums. He listened to "Midnight Train to Georgia," by Gladys Knight, "I Can See Clearly Now" by Johnny Nash, and other songs that made him feel good.

Everyone knew we were a couple and some didn't like it and wanted to break us up. There was one incident that I won't talk about when some devious people drummed up some mess to try to break us up. It broke my heart into a thousand pieces. I was so offended and wounded by the setup I wanted to end my life. I called my best friend Katrina and told her to call Al and tell him to come to the hotel to check on me. When she called him he came right away and took me to the hospital. They pumped my stomach out and released me that same night. He knew how much I loved him and how faithful I was to him. One day, he handed me a note that said, "Nothing or nobody could ever change the way that you feel about me," and he was right. I cherished the note and never threw it away.

We went shopping in Boston, Massachusetts when Al was booked to perform at the Sugar Shack. He bought me a beautiful Calvin Klein double-breasted, eight-button, mink hooded, black cashmere coat. I felt amazing wearing that coat and people complimented me every time I wore it. Both of us loved fashion. Al was one of the best-dressed artists around. When he appeared on the stage, the women went berserk. Some threw their thongs, notes, flowers, and their phone numbers on the stage for him while others tried to rush the stage and jump on it just to touch him. The men were even happy because the women were fired up and ready for some action with their man after the show. Al was the first entertainer to hand out red roses to the women in the audience at his shows. It became his signature. He enjoyed performing as much as he enjoyed buying antique furniture, fine jewelry (diamonds, emeralds, rubies, gold, and other gemstones), and fancy cars. His birthstone is the diamond for the sign of Aries. He read his horoscope every day and believed in astrology. It seemed that he based his day on his daily reading. As a matter of fact, all of us believed in astrology at that time.

Al's family became my surrogate family because I didn't have any relatives or family living in Memphis, TN. His mother was someone I could talk to about my relationship with Al and I could trust her. She knew her son and what he was capable of doing. My relationship with Al did not come without challenges, like most relationships, we had issues. There were times when he had temperament problems and it wasn't a good look, and at other times he was amazing. One warm summer around 2:00 o'clock in the morning we were on the way to Al's house when he started arguing. He threatened to put me out of the car, so I dared him to. He stopped the car and told me to get out. I was shocked that he was going to carry it through. It was nearly pitch dark with the exception of the light of the moon. I sat on the steps of a country store, in the boondocks, and waited for him to turn the car around to come back to pick me up, and he did. Things were beginning to turn sour for us.

We stopped by his mom's house to see her one day when we were on the way to the airport out of town. When we left her house to drive to the airport Al was fussing so he reached down for something in the car and ran into a tree and crashed the car. It was a brand new car that he had bought the night before, a white super beetle Volkswagen with a kit on the front. It was an accident; no one else was around and I thanked God that neither of us was injured. He had a lot of pressure and it affected our relationship. His mom invited me to go with her to church one evening. She asked me if I was baptized, I said yes, and she said that I could get baptized again for repentance. I said ok and was baptized that night. When the mothers of the church circled around me after I came out of the pool, they started to pray and I fell to the floor and started speaking in tongue. I have heard people speaking in tongues, but I never thought or imagined that it would happen to me. Mrs. Green was such a wonderful person, and I am glad I got the chance to spend some time with her. She knew that I loved Al and was loyal to him, and she approved of our relationship.

We traveled to romantic places like Jamaica where I met the Prime Minister and his lovely wife at their home. The island was beautiful. The beaches and clear blue waters were breathtaking. The white sandy beaches and mango trees that lined the streets was a beautiful site to see. The Jamaican people love American music. They remade our songs and gave them a Jamaican beat and feel. I met the infamous Baron Lee, writer, arranger, producer, and owner of the Baron Lee Recording Studio.

Traveling on the road is tiresome and you long for home-cooked meals and a chance to sleep in your own bed. Life on the road is not an easy task. Al fired me one day, so I took a job working at Hot Buttered Soul Limited Recording Studio owned by Isaac Hayes. When Al got wind that I was working for Isaac, he immediately asked me to quit my job working for Isaac and come back to work with him. They were adversaries. Al hired me this time to work from my apartment across the street from the office and study music publishing. I guess eventually I was going to run his publishing company.

I went back to Washington D.C. for short visits. I missed my son James and my family. My son was calling me "Mama Linda." My mom was his mother as far as he was concerned. As the relationship with Al and I became sour and my fairy tale relationship with him was coming to an end, it was the best time for me to think about returning home for good to my son and family. Of course I still was in love with Al but the happiness was gone. Al released a new song after I left, "Call Me," but by that time, our relationship was over. Eventually we reconnected and things were fine but we were not getting back together again as a couple. Whenever he came to the metropolitan area to do a show, I would go to see and support him. He came to DC in 2005 and stayed at my place with me for days. This was around the time he was performing at the Kennedy Center to celebrate the fifth anniversary of 911.

I told him that he should start a cologne line. The idea was good and we moved forward. I designed the bottles and contacted a bottling company in Florida who could mold and make the bottles. That company introduced me to a turnkey company who could manufacture the fragrance, the bottles, labels, and packaging. I engaged a trademark attorney to trademark the name of the cologne line then Al decided not to go forward with the line and aborted the project.

# PART THREE

## WORKING FOR
## TEDDY PENDERGRASS

# CHAPTER SEVEN

## The Road Secretary

In the fall of 1976, I met Teddy Pendergrass at a concert in Washington, D.C. Teddy was a tall, fine, talented brother whose baritone voice gave me chills when I heard him sing. He had a roughness to his voice that was sexy and everyone loved to hear him sing. Henry Evans, Teddy's road manager, invited me to Teddy's party at the hotel after the show. When I arrived dressed in my black leather pants, pull over sweater and black cowboy boots I was ready to party. When I went to Teddy's room he answered the door and asked me to come. When I went into his room it was a far cry from a party. Teddy was the only one there. As I turned around to leave he asked me to stay. He and I talked for hours about the music industry. He told me that he needed a road secretary to travel with him and handle his business on the road right away. He offered me a job that night, but I told him that I would only be available on the weekends to work for him if I decided to go back on the road. Teddy said the weekends would be perfect because it was the only time that he was working. I accepted his offer to work as his road secretary on the weekends. Teddy had recently parted from Harold Melvin, but the Blue Notes went with him. Teddy decided that it was time for a change and moved out the Blue Notes and replaced them with a female backup group, from Houston, Texas.

Philly International Records (PIR), owned by two of my good friends Kenny Gamble and Leon Huff, was to Philly what Motown was to Detroit. Their recording artists included: Patti LaBelle, Billy Paul, Phyllis Hyman, the Jones Girls, Harold Melvin and the Blue Notes, the O'Jays, Jean Carne just to name a few they had a roster of accomplished recording artists. Leon and I were cool and we struck a chord. He was such an interesting person. I clearly remembered one day when he, Walt, and I were in the Fantasy Restaurant in Philly and Teddy walked in. I had dated all three of those guys but at different times in different years. I was supposed to have left Philly to go to DC when I left Teddy's house, but I stopped by the restaurant. I made a beeline out of the restaurant when

Teddy came in because I knew that he was going to show if he saw Walt, Leon and me in the restaurant. Those were the days when I was having the time of my life and hanging out in Philly.

When I was Teddy's road secretary I traveled with him and his band. Those were exciting times. His friends and fans followed him from city to city and came to his hotel to hang out with him because he loved to entertain, I had to be monitor and watch everyone's move in the room just to make sure his valuables were not stolen. Many times I had to put people out of his room. Teddy trusted and depended on me to look out for him and his valuables. He gave me all of his money to keep for him. Some of Teddy's friends came around trying to sell Teddy drugs but I had his money and they couldn't make the sale.

There was always something going on with Teddy. When Teddy performed at Painters Mill, in Baltimore, a theatre in the round, the promoter Dick Clottsman had Teddy's dressing room decorated with balloons and party streamers. I have never seen a dressing room decorated the way Teddy's dressing room was decked out. He was a hell of a promoter. After the show that night many people stopped by Teddy's hotel room to see him. Oprah Winfrey was one of the visitors who stopped to see Teddy. She gave him a chocolate birthday cake shaped like a Teddy bear. Teddy was glad that she stopped by to see him and he offered her a seat and they sat on the sofa alone and talked for a long time while the rest of us were talking and listening to music in the suite. During those days, Oprah was one of the hottest television anchors in Baltimore. Teddy loved the cake that she gave him and he didn't share it with any of us when she left. He took the cake home to Philly the next day to share with his children. One of his regrets was not being a guest on the *Oprah Winfrey Show* after he had his tragic accident. I think he had some things that he wanted to say to Oprah but never got the opportunity.

Teddy was a close friend to Dr. Jay and his wife and one night several car loads of us left Teddy's show in the Meadowlands, New Jersey and drove to the Vice President of Wendy's house. We hung out there for hours before we drove to Philadelphia. Teddy was a friend to celebrities in the music industry. He made sure I was with him on many occasions even after I stopped working for him.

# CHAPTER EIGHT

## Ride or Die Friends

Teddy's manager fired me and told me that he didn't need a road secretary any longer. Even though I was no longer working for him after she fired me, he and I maintained a relationship that no one could break apart. Teddy, Soto, and I rode in Ted's Mercedes Benz to Muhammad Ali's training camp in Deer Lake, PA—outside of Philadelphia. We spent the entire day with the Champ and had dinner with him. Teddy eventually datied one of Ali's ex-wives, and I met her at Teddy's house one day. When Muhammad Ali came to Lanham, MD to fight, I ran into him at the hotel. He made a pass at me and I was flattered LOL. That night I had a ringside seat at the fight and I took pictures with him after he won the fight.

It was a cold winter night in Philadelphia and the ground was covered with snow. Teddy and I had gone to a local bar to have a few cocktails and hang out with his friends. After we left the bar, we got in his car to drive away, but the car stalled. Someone had been tampering with the car because fluid had leaked from the car onto the ground. We got a ride to his house. He found out after the car was towed to the repair shop, that the break line had also been cut. At that point, I realized he had enemies because those things don't occur by happenstance. That was a sign that there was going to be trouble in paradise.

Strange things kept happening to Teddy's other cars. Someone did some major body damage to several of his other cars. He and his security team had to wear bullet proof vests when they went to certain cities. Even though he was nice to me, he had a mean streak and he was very arrogant and nasty to a lot of people. He seldom slept and kept company 24/7 (especially women). His drinking and partying became excessive. His management team, Shep, Danny, and Jeff, did a phenomenal job handling his musical career. Jessie Boseman, concert promoter and friend of Teddy's tried to persuade him to slow down and take some time off and go on vacation. But he didn't listen.

Teddy was scheduled to leave town for a couple of days to tour. His manager accompanied him on some of his trips, but this particular day she stayed behind to handle some business. After she left him, she and some of her staff headed for her home. After they arrived at her house, she got out of the car and walked to her door. From the shadows someone stepped out from behind a bush and shot and killed her. When her mom opened the door, she fell to the floor. When I got the news that she had been killed, I couldn't understand why someone would want to take her life. She and Teddy were in business together but obviously someone wanted her out.

He gave a party at his mansion, formerly owned by Mike Douglas a television host. The record company allegedly bought that house for Ted. The party was invitation only. Many of his celebrity friends, management, and record company executives showed up for the party. There was plenty of delicious food and the finest beverages being served. Music was in the air; his guest were socializing and having a great time, until Teddy pulled a stunt and made a move on me. He made us the center of attention. I had on a two-piece, tight-fitting, rose-colored linen suit and a pair of expensive Charles Jordan shoes—I was clean. He had on a pair of black leather shorts, a white silk shirt and carried a Louie Vuitton pouch in his hand. When he saw me walking across the lawn, he ran over and tackled me to the ground. Everyone stopped in their tracks. It was no secret that he was buck wild, carefree and loved attention. With me, Teddy was playful. He could be himself and not put on airs in front or feel that he was being judged. When Henry, his road manager saw that it was me he said, "Oh, that's Linda Wills; they always play like that." Everyone breathed a sigh of relief. Teddy loved to show me off to his friends as if I were his trophy. He would then dare any one of them to try to date me. He was jealous, spoiled and wanted me for himself.

Teddy began to spiral out of control and his demeanor caused him a lot of grief. He was doing things that I won't even mention in this book, but I sat him down and gave him a reality check several times. Soto couldn't monitor Teddy's every move. Had he been able to, Teddy would have been much more submissive, but Soto did his best to protect him. The pressures of being a superstar along with some other things caused him to drive over the edge. So many people depended on him for their livelihood: his business partners, family, friends, staff, and colleagues. I reminded him constantly about his out of control behavior and disposition. I even wrote him a letter, so he could visualize what his life looked like on paper, and it wasn't a good look. After he read my letter, he told me that he wanted me to be a part of his security team. I told him that it would not be the solution to his problem. He needed to change his attitude and sober up so he could think straight or continue to bear the heavy burden that he was carrying.

Teddy admired my candidness. I kept it one hundred percent with him. When he was wrong I told him he was wrong and why. He knew that I would not blow smoke up his ass like so many of his so-called friends did. They patronized him and he was misled. I didn't want to see my best friend lose his health, dignity, fame, fortune, family, and friends over his foolishness. At times he was pompous and his arrogance bought him a lot of enemies. Teddy fed his appetite with his ego. I told him that I was going to write a book one day and I was going to write about him. He asked me "is it going to be a tell-all book." I told him that his secrets would be safe with me.

Early one morning, I got a phone call from a friend in Philadelphia telling me to come to Philly. Teddy had been in a terrible car accident and was severely injured. I couldn't believe what she was telling me on the other end of the phone. My heart broke into a thousand pieces. I panicked and started to cry. I called my girlfriend Veronica, his close friend, and told her that I was driving to Philly right away. She said that she was going to, so we drove to Philly. Teddy had severed the seventh vertebra in his back, and the doctors couldn't fix it. He was left paralyzed for life. The waiting room was crowded with his friends, family, and enemies. It was alleged by reliable sources that Teddy was moved from the back seat of his Rose Royce to the driver's seat. Before he was moved, he was in the back seat of the car with a woman who was married to a famous man. It was alleged that she got out of the car and into another car that was driving behind them and f led the scene. She did not want to be identified. Teddy was left on the scene with one person. After the media reported the accident, people including my friends started calling him bad names. I was appalled about the way people started talking about him instead of having empathy for him. He could have been killed in that tragic accident. In the 33 years that we have been friends, I have never seen nor heard of him being with another man. People can be jealous, mean and cruel. One minute they are your fans, then the moment they think they have some dirt on you they turn on you. Jealousy is a big time sin and is so unnecessary.

Teddy had to eventually downsize from his 32-room mansion to a smaller house that was handicapped accessible. After he moved into another section of Gladwyne, PA, he got married and I lost contact with him. About a year later, I ran into a friend and she gave me his new phone number. She knew that I had been a close friend to him, and it was important that I reconnect with him. When I called him, he was happy to hear from me. He thought I had abandoned him like so many of his friends, and he started fussing. I told him that when he moved and got married he didn't call me to give me his new phone number. I wasn't trying to get his new number. I wanted him to be happily married. He said, "Look, you have known me long before she came along and I want you to always be around me." I started traveling back to Philly to be with my friend.

Teddy was a generous and warm person when he wanted to be, but he kept his defenses up with certain people for whatever reason. He eventually signed a record deal with a new label and recorded a new album. He began to do concerts again and performed in live stage plays. Things were going well for a while. Then his health took a turn for the worse. His doctor told him that whatever he was doing he needed to stop because it was affecting his health. Teddy was the kind of man who would defy air if he could. He loved a good challenge. He needed people around him who were strong-minded and willed and didn't cater to his every whim.

After being married for ten years Teddy got a divorce. He was good being single for a short time but reality set in and he realized that he needed a wife. His health was declining and he had to stop performing on the road. He told me that he was ready to remarry. His mom was too old to take care of him, and he needed a wife to help around the house and to help take care of him. He couldn't feed himself very well. He had a contraption he tried to use to feed himself, but the food kept falling off of the fork. He preferred someone else to feed him. He had a home nursing service around the clock, and nurses worked in shifts, but still he wanted a wife. He rounded back to old f lames, but none of them were willing to sacrifice their lifestyles to marry a man in a wheelchair. We talked about the possibility of us getting married and what people would say because we were ride-or-die friend. I wasn't up for the challenge and I had a sick mother that I had to take care of in Washington, DC. When I went to Philly to see him, he would set up a date for us to go out to dinner to one of his favorite restaurants. Henry would drive us and wait for us. Ted would kiss me with passion in front of everyone in the restaurant, just showing off.

Eventually he met a woman whom he admired and they started dating. He was pleased with her and everything that she did for him. She showered him with elaborate gifts, prepared exotic meals, dressed him in designer clothes, and showed him love and affection. They married in fewer than two years. He told me he was glad he had finally met a woman who gave to him—he was always giving to others and no one ever gave to him.

Teddy was determined to enhance his revenue stream. He was no dummy and came up with the idea to give a big celebration to commemorate his life and those who helped him survive from his paralyzing car accident. He created Teddy 25: A Celebration of Life, Hope, and Possibilities. When talked about the event in its planning stage, I suggested he consider those whom he wanted to celebrate—his "unsung heroes," such as doctors, nurses, aides, family, and friends. He had lived twenty-five years longer than predicted by his team of doctors. I am sure that his mother, Mrs. Ida Pendergrass, prayed to God and he heard her intercessory prayer for her son's life. Intercessory prayer works if you are a believer.

Teddy 25 was held at the Kimmel Center in Philadelphia, PA on June 7, 2007. It became a whopping success. Many celebrities came out to celebrate and be a part of his event. His gala program consisted of honorees in entertainment— Ashford & Simpson, Kenny Gamble & Leon Huff, Whitney Houston, Cathy Hughes, Patti LaBelle, Mark Mays and Regis Philbin, Mo'Nique, Arthur Fennell (host, CN8/Comcast Network), honorees in medicine; honorees from his career, and honorees of family and friends. The performers and presenters list consisted of Bill Cosby, Julius Erving, Vivian Green, and Kindred the Family Soul, Stephanie Mills, Melba Moore, Musiq Soulchild, Butterball, WDAS radio station, and others. It was a sold-out event. There wasn't an empty seat in the audience. Teddy engaged me to work the backstage area. I identified and escorted his guests to the waiting area in his room. Some of his guests showed up without invitations, but I let them in as well. When the program began, Teddy and his wife were seated on top of the side of the stage. He was dressed in a tuxedo and she in a beautiful gown. It was a black-tie affair and everyone was dressed for the occasion. After the event, I stayed the night at Teddy's house with his family.

His voice started to fade and he could hardly talk much less sing and carry a note. He had developed throat cancer but was cured by surgery. A year or so later, he developed stomach cancer and was told by the doctors that he had a fifty-fifty chance to live if he got the surgery. I asked his wife for permission to visit him in the hospital. I heard she was controlling his visitors list, and I needed to be on the list. I drove to Philly to the hospital to visit him and drove back home after my visit. I tried to cheer him up because Teddy was a free spirit and confinement was hard for him to deal with. He enjoyed my company. He loved to see me dance, so I put on a show and danced for him until both of us fell out laughing. He loved to see me clown.

He had started a non-profit organization "The Teddy Pendergrass Alliance". The mission of the organization was to help and support people with spinal-cord injuries. I made arrangements for him to be a special guest at the Department of Health and Human Services in Washington, DC on a special day when they had a program honoring certain people who had disabilities who were giving back and not giving up. He was proud of his organization and was in the process of getting a physical building to set up shop. When I got the sad news that Ted died, I was grief stricken. I was in New York, celebrating my upcoming birthday and had to rush to Philly to find out what was really going on.

The day of his funeral people came from different parts of the country to celebrate his life. The church was filled from the sanctuary to the balcony with standing room only. Celebrities, clergy, record executives, management, family, fans, friends, and others viewed his body and paid their respects. The line to get into the church was wrapped around the building. At the request of his wife, I was a hostess and helped assist with the guests—to identify them, greet them, and escort them to a waiting area where family and friends gathered before going into the sanctuary for the funeral. The funeral lasted for at least three hours. The wife and family put on a great home going celebration for Teddy. Many songs were song by different artists, speeches and reflections were given by many people well known and not so well known, and the pastor of the church gave the eulogy.

After the funeral the processional line to the cemetery was at least half a mile long. A police escort led the procession. There were two separate repasts: one given by his mother and the other given by his wife. Both repasts were well attended. I went to both of them.

# PART FOUR

# BEHIND THE SCENES IN THE RECORD INDUSTRY

# CHAPTER NINE

## Internship

I was an intern in the music library at WKYS Radio Station. Donnie Simpson was the program director. He approved my internship to work with him in the music library where two other interns were also employed. Jeff Newman was one of the three interns. The radio station was in the same building as the NBC studio on Nebraska Avenue N.W. in Washington, DC. I attended American University (AU) which was located two blocks away from the station. A day in the music library consisted of multitasking, tracking records, answering the phone, compiling lists and reading the trade magazines (Billboard (BB), Radio & Records (R&R), Cashbox, *Jack the Rapper*, *Black Radio Exclusive (BR E)*, *Impact*, and other trade publications).

We consulted with the record pool directors, Eardrum, Wresch, and others to get a list of the records that they were playing and breaking in the clubs. The street (underground) played a role in breaking records. I learned how instrumental and valuable the industry's charts were to the world of entertainment. They were precious, like gold, and all of the record companies and radio stations had subscriptions to the industry periodicals. To an artist, the charts held value and it was important for him to get his record added to the charts. The trades charted all types of music: R&B, pop, jazz, gospel, rap, hip-hop, bluegrass, alternative, house, etc.

While the record promoter was pitching his spiel to the program or music director, I was in the meetings taking it all in and learning the techniques that promotion people used to get a record played. The music library was my training ground for learning promotions. In 1984, I read in *Jack the Rapper* magazine that this music conference was coming in August to Miami, Florida. I booked my flight, made my registrations and flew to Miami to attend the conference. I wanted to become a record promoter and went there to see if I could pick up a couple of accounts. At the record promotions panel session, I asked an all-male panel "How come women were not working as record promoters?" None of the men on the panel answered the question. After the session was over and I was quietly sitting in the lobby, a man walked over to me and said, "So you want to be a record promoter?" He sat beside me and introduced himself as Joe Medlin, one of the greatest record promoters who ever lived. He shared some things about record promotions with me and recommended I contact Roy Ayers about a job as a record promoter for his record company.

# CHAPTER TEN

## Record Promotions

Pepa on the left, me Linda in the middle and Salt on the right

Let me draw the curtain back to give you a glimpse of what goes on behind the scenes with a record promoter. I will walk you thru my journey and give you a brief scenario of some of the artists I have worked with. In 1983, I landed my first account as a record promoter with Uno Melodic Records, owned by Roy Ayers. The mid-Atlantic region was my territory. My major responsibility included promoting records at radio, retail record stores, and nightclubs. Roy's records were easy to work because he was an established artist. I encouraged him to release his song "DC City" as the next single from his album. I knew that I could get plenty of airplay in the mid-Atlantic region and especially in Washington, DC.

I started working for Schwartz Brother's Record and CD Distributor in 1985 as a promotion representative. The amount of records that I had to work compared to Uno Melodic was incomparable. Schwartz was one of the major distributors in the game and they distributed records for independent record companies. Schwartz had branches in different parts of the country. My territory was the mid-Atlantic region where I had a good relationship with the radio station programmers.

Records have to be worked and promoted. Without a promotions rep, it is hard to make a song a hit record and equally as hard to make an artist a superstar. Working records behind the scenes and doing favors in exchange for adds at the stations was commonplace. The rotation (amount of airplay in a day) given to a record (light, medium, heavy or recurrent) is important. The more you hear a song, the better it sounds, and the more you start to like it.

Radio stations are listed by categories; primary (P1) stations and secondary (P2) stations. Many times, it was important for me to go for adds at the P2 stations first because they were the easier adds. When I took a record to a radio station, especially a P1 station, I had to have a story to tell the programmer about the record and it had to be one that would make him want to add the record. It almost always had to do with what other stations were playing in that particular market. Most programmers didn't want to be the first to add a record unless the artist was established and had a track record with a built in audience or if it was a well- known local artist who put out good records and had a following in the market. If Frankie Crocker, superstar New York deejay or Pervis Span in Chicago added a record, a lot of other stations would follow. Stations followed stations in adding records.

When hip-hop music was in its infancy, I was one of the pioneers who promoted hip-hop on radio when it was "unfamiliar" music. I worked all of my genres of music with the same type of enthusiasm and passion. I gave away plenty of promotional CDs and other giveaways to drum up a fan base and potential record buyers. I serviced to the record stores and club deejays as well. I needed the general public sometimes to call the radio stations and make some noise about a certain record. Sometime, when the street speaks, the stations listen. The purpose of a radio station is to ascertain the needs and interests of the community. The demand from the street was felt at the stations by the jammed up request lines. The people were calling the stations day and night requesting songs that they wanted to hear on the radio. Sometimes I had to stage those calls and get my friends and family to call into the station and request a certain song. Whatever I needed to do to get an add, that was lawful, I did. Sometimes, that type of action did force the station to take a chance and play the music.

Week after week, month after month and year after year I promoted records and made a reputation for myself for being a record promoter who could deliver and get records played. I also kept my word with the radio stations; if I told them that I would do something for them, I did it.

Every Tuesday between the hours of 10 am to 2 pm was record day at the radio stations in the mid-Atlantic Region. It was the only day of the week that the programmers met with the record promoters. We lined up in the lobby of the reception area in the radio station and waited our turn to go in and promote our record(s) to the programmer. It was always a huge turnout of record promoters rotating through the doors of the programmer. Sometimes I had an artist with me who was scheduled to go on the air to do a live interview at the stations. At other times the artist came along to meet the programmer so he could establish a future contact or relationship. Record day was the same day in Philly, Baltimore, DC, and VA. Each week I went to different cities for record day. Thursday was the tracking day. It was a day set aside by the programmers to talk to the record promoters on the phone, between the allotted hours. When I tracked a record, I got a status report from the programmer telling me if and when my record would be added to the playlist. In exchange I gave the programmer more information about the status of the record at other stations in or outside of the market. It was certainly not a walk in the park to get some of my records added to the radio stations' playlists.

Schwartz issued me an American Express credit card and an expense account; it helped out tremendously. I was able to take the programmer out for breakfast, lunch, brunch or dinner and use my American Express card to pay for the meals. Every week I had to submit an expense report for the bill that I incurred on my credit card.

Check out my short list and scenario of some of the artists I worked: Al Green, Pendergrass, Roy Ayers, Salt-N- Pepa, Tupac, Doug E. Fresh, EPMD, Jazzy Jeff and Fresh Prince (Will Smith's group), D-Train, Luke, Just Ice, LeVert, Bohannon Jimmy Castor, Mantronics, 2 Live Crew, Timex Social Club, NWA, Tone Loc, Rappin' Duke, H-Town, Betty Wright, George Benson, Bobby Womack, Curtis Mayfield, Smokey Robinson, H. B. Barnum, The Bonner Brothers, Walter Jackson, Johnny Guitar Watson, Jocelyn Brown, Frankie Smith, Johnnie Taylor, Leon Horn, Bobby "Blue" Bland, Clarence Carter, Joyce Simms, Jocelyn Brown, Gene Chandler, Cheryl Lee Ralph, and Essence, among others. Let me give you a bird's eye view of the artist.

H-Town a young R&B group from Houston, Texas had a hit record "Knockin' Da Boots" on the charts. I took the group to Black Entertainment Television to do an interview on "Teen Summit." The three young men were in their mid-twenties. They came protesting about their record company and how they were owed a million dollars and they wanted to collect. They had on white jail jumpsuits, chains bound around their ankles, and handcuffs around their wrists. They made a bold statement with the outfits and went on the air dressed like prisoners. They felt that it was time for them to get a personal manager so they had discussions with me about being the personal manager for the group. Before we could negotiate a deal, Dino, the lead singer was killed in a fatal car accident. After his death, the group broke up. I worked with an eclectic group of artists.

Clarence Carter, an artist who was born blind, had many hit records. I promoted his song "Strokin'" which was a big record. The distributor was selling the record so fast the company couldn't keep it in stock. I didn't have a problem getting his record played because he was known for putting out hit records, and he was an established artist with a track record. I only met him once when he came into the market to do a show.

Jocelyn Brown, on the other hand, was a new artist and she had a big record "Somebody Else's Guy." The radio stations loved the record. She wrote the song and she got some heavy rotation at a lot of the urban stations. I worked directly with her a couple of times and she was ok to work with.

Johnnie Taylor was a pleasure to work with. He was old school and his songs were about relationships. "It's Cheaper to Keep Her," "Whose Making Love," "Somebody's Sleeping in my Bed" were chart busters. He has a great discography of CDs, DVDs and vinyl. It was easy getting adds on Johnnie's songs because his songs were great songs that only needed promotions to break the records in the market. I loved working with Johnnie Taylor; he was such a pro and he talked a lot of trash. Some of the artist that I worked with at Schwartz wrote music scores for movies.

I will tell you about one of the greatest beat boxing hip-hop artists. Doug E. Fresh, Slick Rick, and the Get Fresh Crew were hot in the early 1980's. The group had a two-sided hit record, "The Show" on the A- side and "Ladidadi" on the B-side. The guys wore big, heavy gold rope chains around their necks. Doug dressed in Fila sweat suits and tennis shoes and Fubu jeans and shirts - they were two of his favorite brands that he enjoyed wearing. Doug E loved to beat box (make sounds with his mouth) and was a pioneer in beat boxing. Doug E was also a great rapper and dancer. His dance became a dance craze in the country.

Slick Rick (aka Rick the Ruler) wore a patch over one of his eyes and it usually matched his outfit. Rick had his own style of dress. He wore and was known for wearing mounds of big heavy jewelry. He was originally from Mitcham London, England but he grew up in the Bronx in New York.

When Doug and Rick performed at the Capital Center Puffy was a student at Howard University. Puffy would come to the shows and dance on stage with Doug. Puffy had the gift of dance and he was an excellent rapper. What I noticed the most about Puffy was what he was wearing on his head. To me it looked like a weird hat. When I asked him one day why he was always wearing the hat that he had on, he said, "It's not a hat, it's a crown that my mom makes and sells in New York." Wow, little did Puffy or his mom know that Puffy would be crowned and honored for his brilliance and innovation to the music industry.

Gerald LeVert, Eddie LeVert's son, had a group called LeVert and they were signed to Harry Coones record label. Harry was a former executive at Philadelphia International Records. Harry and I rode in a snow blizzard to Petersburg, Virginia to get the first add on LeVert's new song "I'm Still." I had a good working relationship with the program directors and he promised me the add if I got the record to him. So I drove my car and got the record to him and he kept his promise and added the record. When the group came to DC, for a short promotional tour, I picked them up from the airport and drove them around in my car; the label didn't pay for a limousine for them, but we had a good photographer Oggie. All of the promotion reps used Oggie as their photographer. I took the group to a radio station in the market to do a live air interview. Then I took them to a couple of record stores to do in-stores and sign autographs. After the record gained some momentum and recognition in the country, Gerald signed a solo deal with Atlantic records. I have also worked with new and legendary artists like Walter Jackson.

It was a pleasure working with the legendary Walter Jackson. He was crippled, with polio as a child and he walked on crutches. As a former member of the Velvetones, he was discovered by the A & R man for Columbia Records and was later signed to a deal as a solo artist. He has a discography of hits like: "What Would You Do," "Welcome Home," "Speak Her Name," and more. Walter was a balladeer singer and his voice was smooth and sultry. I enjoyed working with and talking to him. He was friendly and one of the nicest artists that I have worked with. Some of the other artists that I worked with had novelty songs.

Jimmy Castor and the Jimmy Castor Bunch was a funk soulful disco group. They recorded songs like "Everything Man, the E-Man," "Troglodyte," "Bertha Butt Boogie," and other great songs. They were a popular group for many years, and many other artists have sampled their music. Jimmy was a pleasure to work with and I enjoyed working his records. Just like Jimmy Castor there was the Rapping Duke who had a novelty song.

Shawn Brown, a hip- hop artist, had a record called "The Rapping Duke." The concept of the song mimicked the movie actor John Wayne. The dah-ha, dah-ha was a caricature of John Wayne's voice. His record peaked at 73 on the Hot R&B/hip-hop billboard chart. The radio stations played the song because it was fun, and it was different. The artist that I am going to talk about next wrote music scores for movies.

The legendary Curtis Mayfield singer, writer, arranger, producer, and owner of Custom Records, was formerly a member of the group, "The Impressions." I was honored to meet Curtis and work his records. He was an established artist and his records were easy to work and get adds at the radio stations. Curtis was self-contained and wrote for himself, the Impressions, and others. Curtis also played the guitar. People, that Cat had a voice on him that was next to none. Curtis was soft spoken, and he was a gentle person. We spent quality time together when he was in the market and we established a good working relationship.

What can I say; I have worked with so many celebrities. Bobby Womack was another of my favor artists to work with. He was funny and kept me laughing. His records were easy to promote and got added on the radio stations because he was self-contained and he wrote hit after hit. He also played the guitar. When Bobby performed at the Capital Center I was with him as his promotion rep. He introduced me to Mick Jagger and the Rolling Stones; they were on the same show. Mick Jagger invited Bobby Womack to come to his hotel after the show to see him; they were friends. We went by Mick's room after the show.

Speaking about legends George Benson, a vocalist and guitarist had a record on an independent label. I worked the record in my markets, and it did well at radio. As a part of his promotion tour, I took him to an after party at the Fox Trap, a well-known upscale club in D.C. George is really a shy person, but he was cordial with the people and he signed some autographs. He gave me a bouquet of flowers that night as his appreciation for the work that I did on his record.

Next, I am going to introduce you to two of the legendary men who wrote many hit songs for Motown Records. Brian and Eddie Holland, brothers from the team Holland Dozier Holland, came to DC to visit Schwartz Brothers. I rode in the limo with the guys to a couple of radio interviews and assisted them at an event that night. They were very nice men and they shared a wealth of history about Motown Records.

To my surprise, I was working a record for Cheryl Lee Ralph, movie actress. Cheryl had a record out on an independent label but it didn't catch on with the programmers because I think they stereotype people. For them she was in the movie business and not in the record business. That's just my professional guess as to why they didn't play her record. I got a chance to meet her when she came to Schwartz Brothers to meet with Steve Schwartz and the staff.

After working the streets and hitting the road promoting records it was that time of year when the music conferences were held and I was ready to go. I can go on for days talking about the artists that I have worked with, but now I want to give you some digs about the music conferences; Jack the Rapper, Impact, Black Radio Exclusive, Urban Network, Black Music Association, and more.

The music conferences were fun and off the chain. Schwartz Brothers usually had a suite at the music conferences. Voo Doo, my co-worker and me, hosted the parties in the suite for the company. We decorated the room with our artist flats, posters and pictures which made the room look festive. We had plenty of food, beverages, and giveaways for our guests. I had to register, some of our artists from various record companies for the conference and they had to come to me in the suite to get their credentials and gift bags. The record companies and affiliates supplied the gifts for the gift bags. The gift bags were a big-ticket item at the music conferences and could disappear in the blink of an eye if you didn't keep up with them. The bags were stuffed with books, records, CDs, t-shirts, posters, pictures, cosmetics; whatever gifts that were donated from companies were put in the bags. It was a fun time for all of us at the music conferences. It was also a good place and time to network.

All of the music conferences were well attended organized and patronized by the major and independent record companies. The new artists' showcases helped the new artists gain some notoriety. There were panel sessions, concerts, meet and greets, receptions, Q&A sessions, golf tournaments and a host of other things all packed into a fun filled three-days at all of the conferences. Most of the conferences were closed to the public. The awards dinner was always the highlight of the conference. Around that time, the superstars show up to receive their awards and make their acceptance speeches. The front of the hotel looked like a parking lot for the rich and famous with several Rolls Royce, Bentleys, Limousines, town cars, vans, limousine buses, etc. The artists and record companies had great expectations of me as their representative in the markets.

Some of the places, where I had to go, to drop off the records, at radio stations or clubs were not always safe places to go. Some of the places were greasy spoons, as we term them in the music industry, in rough neighborhoods, where garbage and trash littered the streets. Then you had the drug addicts loitering on the street corners making it unsafe for a stranger like me to walk pass them for fear of being assaulted or robbed. However, it was par for the course.

When I left Schwartz Brothers, I got a job working as the Northeast Regional Promotions Representative for SBK Records at their CEMA branch, in Lanham, Maryland. SBK was a major record label and had a variety and number of recording artists signed to the label (country singer Garth Brooks, pop singer Wilson Phillips, R&B Riff singers, alternative, and hip-hop Vanilla Ice rapper just to name a few).

Smokey Robinson was one of the R&B artists on the record label that I had the pleasure to work with. I promoted his record "Double Good Everything" at the urban stations, but it didn't quite appeal to the programmers, like we thought it would. The company thought that since Smokey had such an excellent reputation for releasing and singing great records, we thought that it would be a shoe in to get his record played, but it was quite the contrary. Smokey's familiar sound was the Motown sound, and he was stereotyped by the programmers and his fans; they wanted the Motown sound from him.

Vanilla Ice was signed to SBK as a hip-hop artist. He was the first white person to make it as a successful rapper in the hip-hop world. The one problem that I had with Ice was trying to wake him up on time one morning, so he could make his flight on time. I knocked on his door for at least ten minutes before he answered. His record "Ice Ice Baby" became a big hit record and it did well on the music charts. His stage performance was good with his dancing and background dancers. He had a promising career in the music industry.

Riff, an all male R&B group from Patterson, NJ was one of the R&B groups signed to SBK. They played in the movie *Patterson High* starring Morgan Freeman. Their role in the movie landed them a record deal with SBK records. All of them were good singers and they had a future in the music industry and they sold a lot of records. I enjoyed working with them. I like helping young artists come up in their musical careers.

SBK had their annual sales meeting in Palm Springs, Florida. We had mandatory meetings to attend every day. The meetings were interesting and I learned a lot. They showcased new artists and everyone mingled and established relationships. We learned about the direction that the company was headed for the future. Early in the morning, before going to meetings, I sat outside on my balcony and watch the beautiful, colorful sailboats go by. Palms Springs, Florida is a beautiful and enchanting place.

When SBK merged with the EMI group, all of us were caught up in the RIFF, reduction in the work force. The company downsized and we were paid a severance pay and referred to Head Hunters, a temp agency that would help us to find new jobs. I went back to working as an independent.

Next Plateau became one of my main accounts. I have fostered a working relationship with them through Schwartz Brothers. Salt-n-Pepa, Sybil, Kings of Pressure, Red Alert, O.C. and Crazy Eddie from the Fearless Four, were some of the hip hop artists I promoted. I spent more time working directly with Salt-n-Pepa. I always knew that they were going to become superstars in the entertainment industry. The group was born for the stage. Those young ladies were relevant, current, excellent rappers, performers, and dancers; they were trendsetters. No female group, at that time, could match them on stage. I introduced them to go-go style of music when they came into the DC area. They met Sugar Bear from EU and recorded a record together "Shake Your Thing," and the song became a hit record and was on Salt-n-Pepa's CD. It has been a decade or so and Salt-n-Pepa are still going strong and selling out shows. Next Plateau presented me with a gold record and CD, with my name engraved on the plaque to commemorate the sale of more than five hundred thousand copies sold of Salt-n-Pepa's album and CD, "Hot, Cold and Vicious."

Working for Doug E. Fresh was great. I got a chance to live and work in New York during the week. I commuted from DC on Monday mornings to New York City on the train and was back out on Friday nights or early Saturday mornings. At the time, I was attending a local university on the weekends studying for my masters degree in marketing. Doug's office was located downtown in Manhattan at Gee Street Records. As the Business Manager I handle the day-to-day issues. I negotiated contract, built and maintained relations with his clients. Londell McMillian Esquire was Doug E.'s lawyer at that time. I handled his affairs pertaining to his music career and traveled, scheduled meetings and appointments.

Doug was quickly rising to the top and establishing his brand. The radio stations play both sides of his A and B records (La Di Da Di and The Show);he had a two sided hit record. The public and the media were onboard. Doug E. was hot and his music rang out across the country and I believe it crossed over to the pop chart. His show was filled with plenty of energy and excitement. His dance became a dance craze. Doug had business dealings with Nike, Fubu, and other brands. He loved to wear the Fubu and Fila Gear. Doug also asks me to call Swiss Beatz for tracks for him. Beatz is now married to Alicia Keyes.

After Doug moved his office from Gee Street, we had our weekly staff meetings at Chill Will's house and we discussed show dates, the rider, tour support, BDS radio spins, office supplies, and other company matters. I had subscribed to the trade magazines to keep abreast of the latest trends in the business and to keep up with the chart numbers on his records. Since I was attending college on the weekends studying to get my masters of business administration in marketing and Doug closed his office at Gee Street, I was able to work from home in my office in DC for Doug E. Fresh Entertainment.

When the Million Man March was held in Washington, DC, Doug brought his family to Washington to attend the march. With him was his wife, Gee Gee; his four sons Daquan, Solomon, Chem, and Joshua; his brother-in-law Nicholas, and father Hammurabi Bey. I would be remissed, if I didn't mention Jonah, Doug's youngest son, but he wasn't born at that time. Everyone stayed at my place that night. My grandson, Delonte' was at the house with us. Even though it was crowded in my one bedroom apartment, we cooked, talked, watched television, and had a good time. The next morning, we got up, ate breakfast, got dressed, and walked to the National Mall to the march. When we got on the mall we had to walk the crowd of people and I led the way. We climbed the stairs to the top of the Capitol landing where the guests gathered. Minister Farrakhan, Mrs. Coretta Scott King, Russell Simmons, Puffy, Whitney Houston, Bobby Brown, Blacks in Government, and other entertainers and celebrities were there.

The weather was perfect for a march and it certainly was a day of harmony. There was a massive crowd of different ethnicities who gathered and marched peacefully on the National Mall in the Nation's Capital. It was an amazing historic day for the African Americans in this county. We stood together in solidarity for a common cause, one and a half million people, gathered in one place. Doug E and his family, all of us, enjoyed the march. We were glad that we supported the march. The next day our pictures were in the *Recall* newspaper.

Sleeping Bag and Fresh Records were my major accounts and I had great repore with Ron Resnick, one of the owners. They gave me a personalized gold record with my name engraved on the plaque for EPMD's CD "Strictly Business," that sold a million copies. The record company gave a rooftop soirée in downtown Manhattan and invited me up to New York to attend the party. They had servers walking around with food trays, top shelf liquor, and entertainment. The smell of food was in the air and everyone was having a ball. Three weeks later I was on an all-expense paid trip to London, England. Sleeping Bag Records sponsored my entire trip. When I arrived at the Heathrow airport, a chauffeur in a Rolls Royce car picked me up and drove me to the hotel. The car had a white animal-skin scatter rug on the floor, and the bar was full of drinks. I was living the rock and roll lifestyle and with first-class treatment; it felt amazing. When I arrived at the hotel, I had to show my passport to the clerk at the desk and then sign my name in a huge logbook. I stayed at the Hyde Park Hotel overlooking Hyde Park.

The next day the group EPMD came to London with Ron Resnick. I hung out with the guys for a couple of days. We went to Piccadilly Circle one day to check out the designer stores and I bought a London Fog trench coat. The following day I went sightseeing. At night, the doors in the hall in the hotel would swing back and forth, making squeaky noises like a haunted house. It was a spooky and creepy scene. I went to Redding, England the night before I left England and hooked up with the group Stetsosonic at a club. They were signed to Fresh Records and were doing a tour in England. I eventually went back to working independent and worked for several independent record companies.

I worked the mid-Atlantic region for Luke Records (aka Luther Campbell) for several months, as a promotion representative. H-Town and the 2-Live Crew were two of the hottest groups signed to Luke records at that time. Luke started the trend of using strippers on stage to dance, as a part of his show and they turned it up each time. Luke had a party one night at a conference and his dancers were dancing on the bed in the room and on the tables and they were everywhere. I politely left the room; it was no place for me. Working with him taught me humility. Luke was the kind of boss who didn't have any cut cards and expressed himself to his staff however he saw fit. When I left his record company I started working for Maverick Records.

Ed Strickland the national promotion representative for Maverick Records (Madonna's company) hired me to work Tupac Shakur's record in the Washington, DC market. At that time, Tupac had left the group Digital Underground to become a solo artist. He had a new song called "Brenda's Got a Baby" which became his first hit record as a solo artist. Tupac was a friendly, energetic young man and he loved to laugh and smile. We talked about the things that mattered to him the most, his sister and his childhood. Pac and his sister had to take turns washing the dishes when they were growing up, and it was something that he hated doing. He would bargain with his sister to wash the dishes for him on his day and promised to take care of her once he became famous. Tupac was a conscious rapper and everyone enjoyed his lyrical storytelling style. His record company wanted a limousine service to take his around town when he arrived in DC so I hired a limousine company. I rode with Pac in the limo and we got a chance to bond.

I started Wills Entertainment became the personal manager for many artist and taught them how to copyright their music at the Library of Congress. I decided to start my own publishing company (Right Shoe and Left Shoe).

# CHAPTER ELEVEN

## Conclusion

I've learned to work as a team player by growing up in a normal family setting as a child, with a mother, father and sibling living together as a unit. I learned how to socialize, share, and take responsibility and accountability for my actions and my life's successes. Even though I was worn down from my losses, tragedies and disappointments, I've learned to weather the storm and keep things moving in a positive manner.

I fell in love with the man of my dreams—a superstar and that dream became a reality. I was afforded an opportunity to work behind the scenes in the music industry as a record promoter and enhanced the lives of many artists who went on to become superstars from the fruits of my labor.

Learning the music business has shaped and molded my career path and life. I was presented with many gold record awards from the record companies, gained a wealth of knowledge, and made contacts with many prestigious people in the record industry.

As a pioneer record promoter, who promoted hip-hop when hip-hop wasn't popular as we know it today, I feel honored by that accomplishment. Hip-hop is a culture and lifestyle shared by people around the world. I succeeded on all fronts promoting R&B, jazz, gospel, blues and rap, hip-hop and go-go music. I believe I made my contribution to the history of black music.

# Praise For Linda Wills

"My niece, Linda Wills, is one of the bright spots of our family. The sky is the limit for her, and she is a winner. She will make mistakes and take risk for her future."

—Maury Wills, Los Angeles Dodgers MVP

"Linda Wills is a living treasure, with an endless wealth of knowledge to share, from her many real life experiences and beyond. She will always be family."

—Doug E. Fresh, Hip-Hop Artist

"Linda Wills was not only a Record Promoter, but she was also the Record Promoters' Promoter. She was always a woman of her word.
Whenever she said she was going to do something for a radio station – you could totally count on it."

— Cathy Hughes, Founder of Radio and TV One

"Linda Wills was not only an amazing promotions expert, she was always a gracious hostess and friend to all the artists she worked with. She always handled her business with class and made it look easy. It was always a pleasure working with her. She still comes to see us when we play in DC or nearby cities, and we are always happy to see her. Linda Wills is a strong woman with an awesome testimony. She is a survivor and an inspiration."

—Salt-n-Pepa, Rappers

"Linda is one of the best of the best. She is probably the best promotion manager in the world. She is my girl, and I really appreciate her as well as her work ethics."

—Roy Ayers, jazz artist and musician

"Linda Wills is deeply rooted in the music scene in the District, Virginia, and Maryland (DVM)…from R&B to Rap, Hip-Hop and Go-Go music. She has dedicated her career to support many and was responsible for breaking Hip Hop music when no one understood or believed. She is a woman with perseverance and integrity."

—Darryll Brooks, CD Productions

"My sister, Linda, is one ambitious, admirable, and amazing woman. She is second to none, my one and only sister. God's favor is upon her life. I love you, Linda!"

—Pastor Mark Wills, brother

"Thank God for Linda and her contributions to the community of the arts. She has been influential in the achievement of a great number of people. As her pastor, I appreciate Linda being true to the faith, always willing to partner and participate for the cause of Christ. Paul talks about Timothy knowing his faith and where his faith came from—his mother and grandmother. I reference Paul to say of Linda that I know where her faith came from: her wonderful and kind hearted mother (Elaine), whom, we miss dearly. God bless you, my sister, in yet another endeavor that will yield much fruit to your account. 'Only what you do for Christ will last.'"

— Louis B. Jones II, Pastor

# INDEX

## A

African Americans, 5, 12–15, 18, 24, 62
ANC (Advisory Neighborhood
    Commissioner), 18–19
AU (American University), 17–18, 51
Ayers, Roy, ix, xii, 54–55, 66

## B

Baltimore, 30, 42, 55
Banneker Field, 11
Barnum, H. B., xii, 55
Baron Lee Recording Studio, 36
Barry Farms, 3, 5
Benson, George, 58
Beverly Hills, 32
Bland, Bobby "Blue," 55, 58
Blue Notes, 41
Bonner Brothers, 55
Boseman, Jessie, 43
BRE (Black Radio Exclusive), 51
Brooks, Darryll, 66
Brown, Jocelyn, 55–56

## C

Capital Center, 57–58
Capitol, 62
Carol (friend), 27–28

Carter, Clarence, 55–56
Castor, Jimmy, 57

## D

Doug, Fresh E., 56–57, 61
Doug E. Fresh Entertainment, 61

## E

Enterprise Band, 29–30, 34

## F

Farrakhan (minister), 62
Fresh, Doug E., ix, xii, 55–56, 61, 65

## G

Gee Street Records, 61
Get Fresh Crew, 56
Green, Al, 27–37
Green Enterprises, 31

## H

Hayes, Isaac, 36
Henry (road manager), 15, 44, 46
Holland Dozier Holland, 58

Hot Buttered Soul Limited
    Recording Studio, 36
Howard Theatre, 14–15
H-Town, xii, 55–56, 63
Hughes, Cathy, 65

**I**

Ingram, Oliver, 27–29, 31

**J**

Jagger, Mick, 58
Jamaica, 31, 36
John, Elton, 32
Jones II, Pastor Louis B., 66

**K**

King, Martin Luther, 12–13

**L**

LeVert, Eddie, 57
LeVert, Gerald, xii, 57
London, 33, 62
Luke (record-label owner), xii, 55, 63

**M**

Mayfield, Curtis, 55, 58
Medlin, Joe, 52
Memphis, 13, 29–30, 32, 35
Miami, 51
Million Man March, 61
MVP (Most Valuable Player), 11, 21

**N**

New York City, 29, 61

**P**

Pendergrass, Teddy, xii, 39, 41
Pentagon, 19–20
Philadelphia, 42–43, 45
Precola DeVore Charm and
    Modeling School, 19
Priddy, Gerry, 10

**R**

Ralph, Cheryl Lee, 58
Robinson, Smokey, 60
*R&R* (*Radio & Records*), 51

**S**

Salt-n-Pepa, ix, xii, 60–61, 65
SBK Records, 60
Schwartz Brothers, 54–56, 58–60
Slick Rick, 56–57
Soto (bodyguard of Ted), 43–44
Stones, Rolling, 58

**T**

Taylor, Johnnie, 55–56
Ted, 43–44, 46–47
Tupac, 55, 63

**U**

Uno Melodic Records, 53

# W

Washington Hospital Center, 22
White House, 14–15, 23
Wills, Cornell (brother), 3, 17, 22, 30
Wills, Everett (brother), 21–22, 24
Wills, Jamie (brother), 9
Wills, Mark (brother), 24
Wills, Maury (uncle), 10–11
Wills, Melvin (brother), 23, 29
Winfrey, Oprah, 42
Womack, Bobby, 55, 58
Wonder, Stevie, 18

Made in the USA
Middletown, DE
19 March 2023